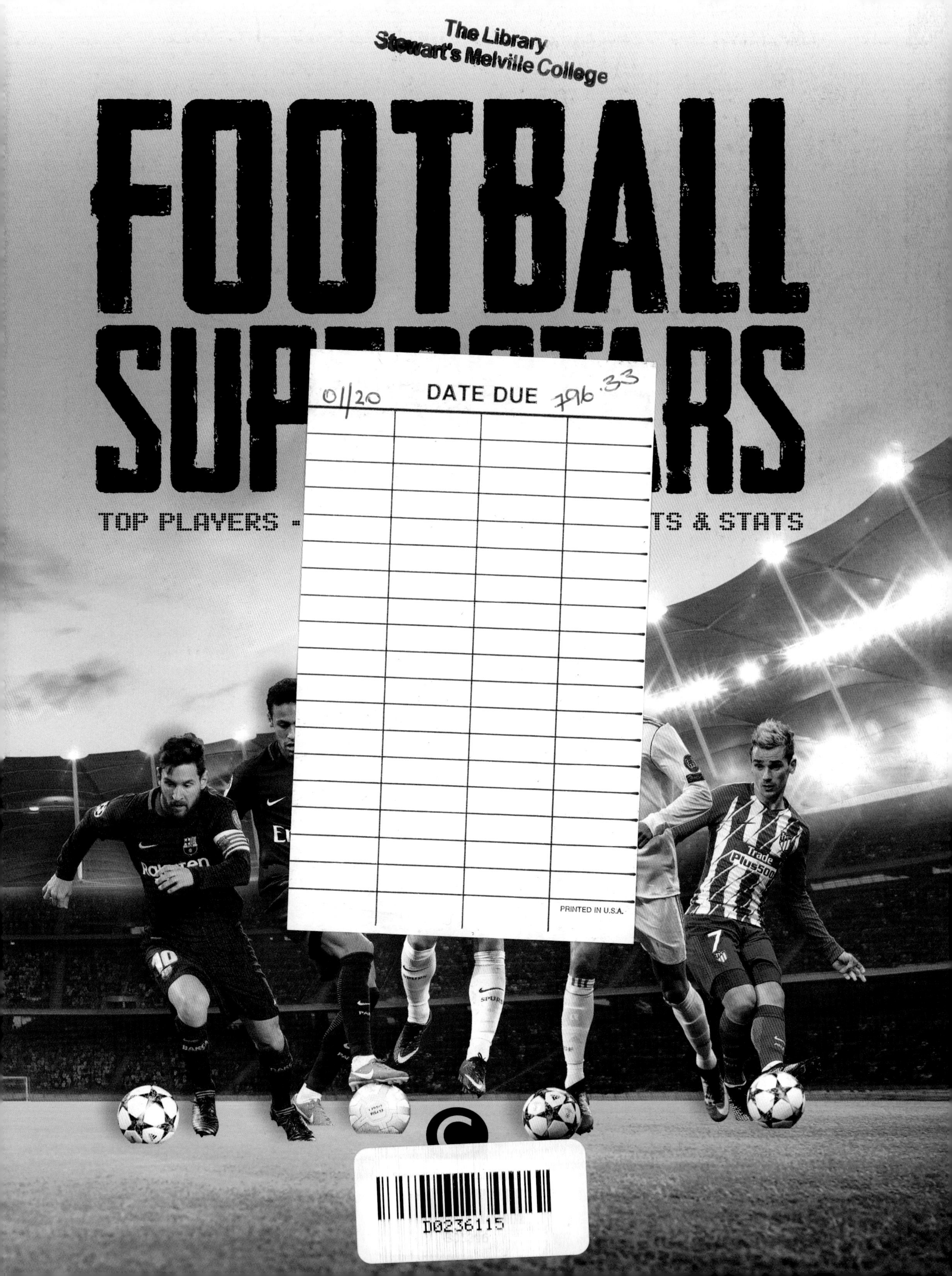
The Library
Stewart's Melville College
FOOTBALL
SUP
ARS
TOP PLAYERS -
TS & STATS
01/20
DATE DUE
796.33
PRINTED IN U.S.A.
D0236115

# CONTENTS



Note to readers: the facts and statistics in this book are accurate as of 25 February 2018.

# STARS OF THE GAME

Welcome to **FOOTBALL SUPERSTARS**, a celebration of the hottest players in world football right now. This collection features **25 LEGENDS OF THE GAME** from superb keepers to explosive strikers – there's no one you wouldn't want in your squad.

Learn how each player started out, his skills, clubs and how his talent took him to the top. Plus find out all the **FACTS AND STATS** to wow your friends. A chapter on the young stars currently taking the game by storm completes our collection. Pick your tip for a future Ballon d'Or winner, then tackle our **FIENDISH QUIZ** to test your knowledge of all the pro players.

## PLAYERS AND STATS

The player profiles give you the lowdown on each player's career so far – appearances, goals and trophies won. Whose trophy cabinet is bulging the most? Which players have scored season after season, made the most assists or set special records? Compare the stats and choose your first XI.

Real Madrid legends Toni Kroos, Marcelo and Sergio Ramos celebrate another goal for *Los Blancos*.

# SUPERSTARS DREAM TEAM

While reading this book, think about which players would make it into your dream team. Fill in the player names on the left and put them in position on the pitch.

| PLAYER NAME | SHIRT |
|---|---|
| | |
| | |
| | |
| | |
| | |
| | |
| | |
| | |
| | |
| | |
| | |

# SERGIO AGÜERO

Manchester City's all-time **LEADING GOALSCORER**, Agüero made his professional debut at just 15 years and 13 days old, for Argentinian club Independiente. He set a new record for the **YOUNGEST PLAYER** in the league. The exceptional forward has continued to **SMASH RECORDS** throughout his footballing career.

## MANCHESTER CITY

### FORWARD

**FULL NAME:** Sergio Leonel Agüero
**NICKNAME:** Kun (named after a cartoon character)
**DATE OF BIRTH:** 2 June 1988
**PLACE OF BIRTH:** Buenos Aires, Argentina
**HEIGHT:** 1.73m **WEIGHT:** 69kg
**LEFT OR RIGHT FOOTED:** Right
**SQUAD NUMBER:** 10
**INTERNATIONAL TEAM:** Argentina

## SPANISH SWITCH

In May 2006, Agüero joined Spanish club Atlético Madrid from Independiente for a club-record fee of around £19.5 million. By 2010, he had scored 101 goals in 234 appearances for the Red and Whites, while winning the UEFA Europa League and UEFA Super Cup. Europe's richest clubs competed for his signature and Agüero moved to Manchester City in July 2011 for a fee thought to be around £35 million.

## ARGENTINE HERO

Agüero made his debut for Argentina's senior side in 2006 at the age of 18. A gold medal at the 2008 Olympics, alongside appearances at the 2010 FIFA World Cup and 2011 Copa America established Kun as a permanent fixture. His sharp shooting, acceleration and strength have helped him to hit the back of the net 36 times for Argentina.

## SUPER SKY BLUE

Agüero enjoyed a superb first season in England, scoring twice on his City debut, and ending the season with 30 goals overall. He cemented his place in City's history when he scored a dramatic goal in the 94th minute on the last day of the 2011–12 season, finally ending the club's 44-year wait for the league title. A second Premier League title plus a League Cup win came in 2013–14, with Agüero netting 28 goals for the Sky Blues. The following season saw him notch up his 100th Premier League goal. He is the most successful striker from South America ever to appear in the Premier League.

**Agüero makes up an awesome forward line for Argentina alongside Lionel Messi.**

## FOOTIE FACT

***Agüero broke Eric Brook's club record for Manchester City when he scored in a 4–2 win at Napoli in October 2017 to move on to 178 goals. The previous record had stood for 77 years.***

# DELE ALLI

It's incredible to think that Alli has played only three full Premier League seasons, yet has already established himself as one of Europe's **MOST WANTED** players. The pacy, attacking midfielder was a **BARGAIN** for Spurs at just £5 million – he's now worth around **£130 MILLION** and is firmly on the radar of giants Real Madrid and Barcelona.

## TOTTENHAM HOTSPUR

### ATTACKING MIDFIELDER

**FULL NAME:** Bamidele Jermaine Alli

**NICKNAME:** Bam Bam

**DATE OF BIRTH:** 11 April 1996

**PLACE OF BIRTH:** Milton Keynes, England

**HEIGHT:** 1.88m **WEIGHT:** 79.5kg

**LEFT OR RIGHT FOOTED:** Right

**SQUAD NUMBER:** 20

**INTERNATIONAL TEAM:** England

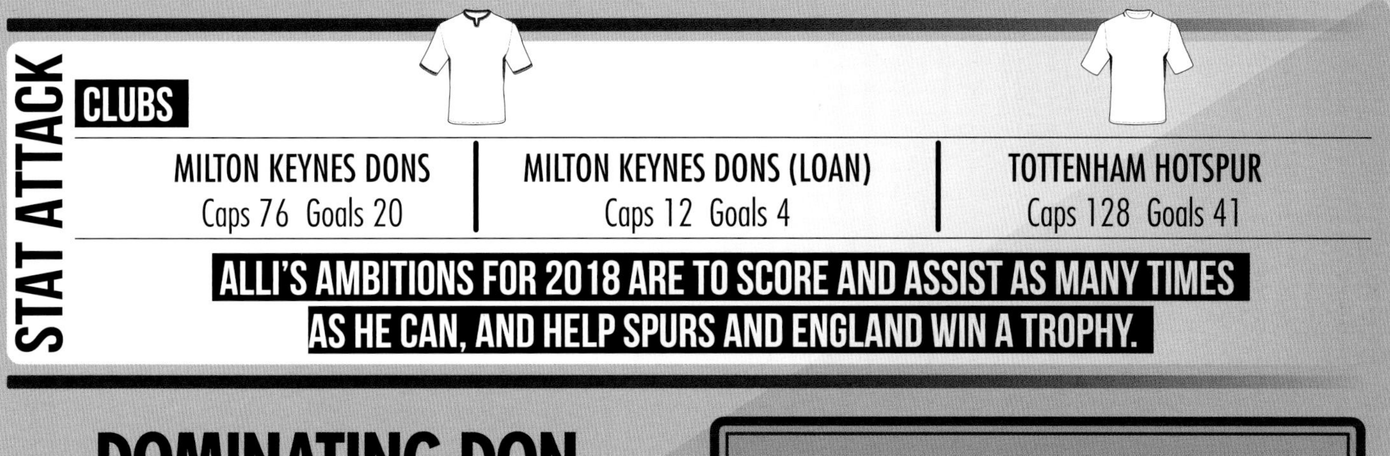


## DOMINATING DON

Alli's first professional club was MK Dons – his home town team – which he joined at the age of 11. He was part of the Dons side that beat Manchester United in a 4–0 League Cup win back in 2014 – a famous victory for the lowly League 1 team. His big-match performances and eye-catching goals attracted scouts from across Europe. At the end of the January 2015 transfer window, Alli signed for £5 million with Spurs, but was loaned back to the Dons for the rest of the season.

## LEADING LION

Alli's form for England has matched his impressive club record. Man-of-the-match performances and a brilliant long-range goal in his first start against France have ensured Dele is one of the first names on manager Gareth Southgate's team-sheet. A tie against Messi's Argentina or Iniesta's Spain would be the biggest test of Alli's career to date.

## HOT SPUR

Alli made his Spurs debut in August 2015. Some stunning performances and wonder goals early on earned him a new contract and he finished his debut campaign with ten league goals. The 2016–17 season saw Dele deliver some deadly finishes, scoring 22 goals in all competitions, as Spurs made a charge for the Premier League title. They eventually finished third, but Alli was named in the Premier League Team of the Year and was voted Young Player of the Year for the second season in a row.

Alli could have chosen to play for Nigeria, as his father comes from the west African country.

## FOOTIE FACT

***Alli chooses to wear 'Dele' on the back of his shirt instead of his surname after a difficult time growing up.***

# PIERRE-EMERICK AUBAMEYANG

African forward Aubameyang has developed into one of the **DEADLIEST STRIKERS** in world football – his combined **SPEED AND FINISHING** are a danger to any defence. The French-born striker chose Gabon as his national team to help put his country and **AFRICAN FOOTBALL** on the map. His footballer father, Pierre, was a former Gabon captain and one of the country's first players to play in Europe.

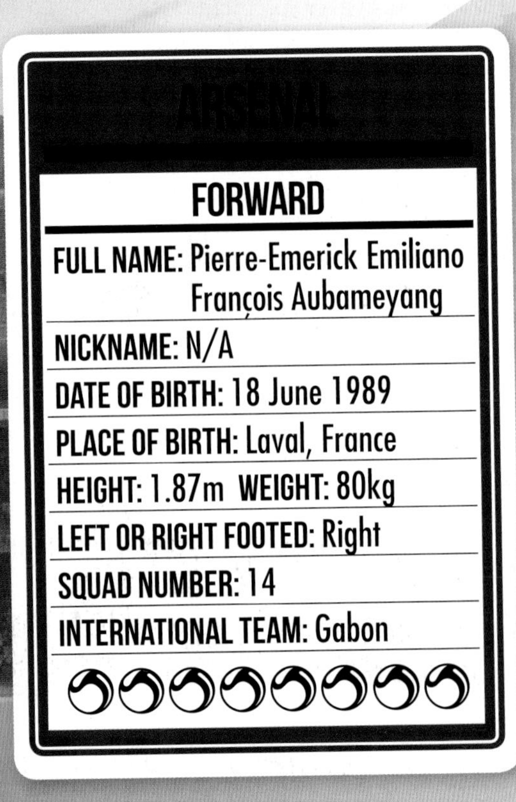
ARSENAL

FORWARD

FULL NAME: Pierre-Emerick Emiliano François Aubameyang
NICKNAME: N/A
DATE OF BIRTH: 18 June 1989
PLACE OF BIRTH: Laval, France
HEIGHT: 1.87m WEIGHT: 80kg
LEFT OR RIGHT FOOTED: Right
SQUAD NUMBER: 14
INTERNATIONAL TEAM: Gabon

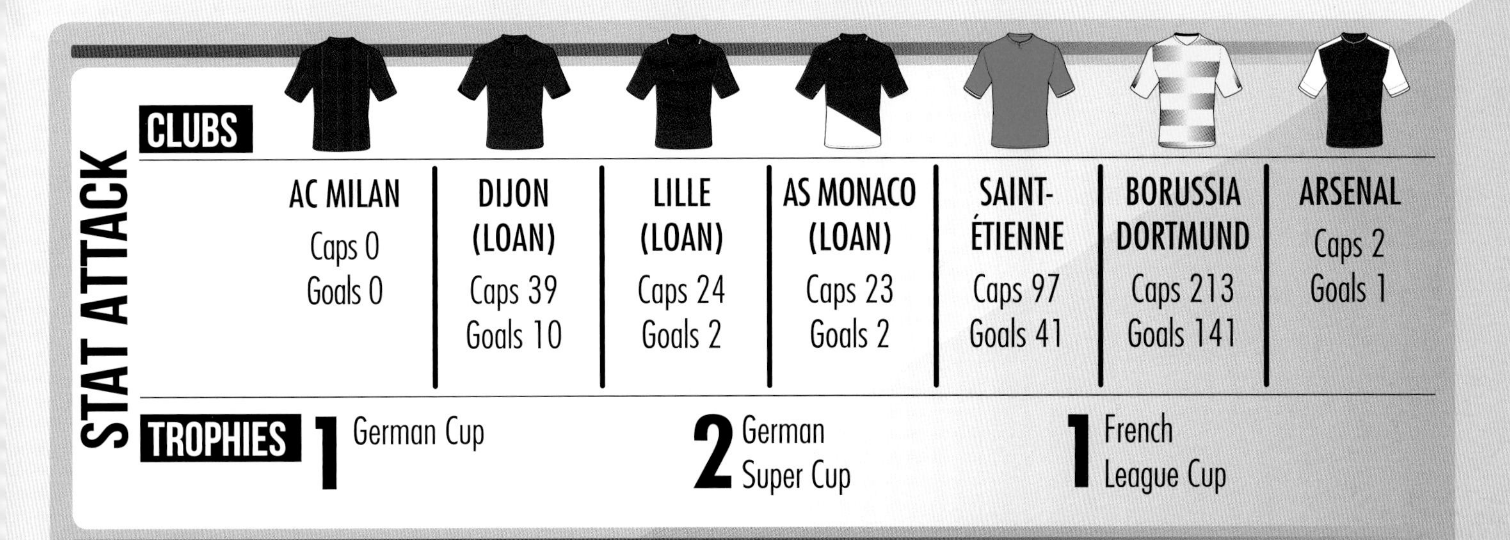

STAT ATTACK

CLUBS

| AC MILAN | DIJON (LOAN) | LILLE (LOAN) | AS MONACO (LOAN) | SAINT-ÉTIENNE | BORUSSIA DORTMUND | ARSENAL |
|---|---|---|---|---|---|---|
| Caps 0 | Caps 39 | Caps 24 | Caps 23 | Caps 97 | Caps 213 | Caps 2 |
| Goals 0 | Goals 10 | Goals 2 | Goals 2 | Goals 41 | Goals 141 | Goals 1 |

TROPHIES

1 German Cup

2 German Super Cup

1 French League Cup

## FAMILY TIES

A young Aubameyang signed for AC Milan in 2007, the club where his father was a scout and his two brothers, Catilina and Willy, tried – and failed – to make their names. But with legendary strikers Ronaldinho, Andriy Shevchenko and Filippo Inzaghi already in the team, Pierre-Emerick was sent out on loan, playing for a series of French clubs. In Ligue 1, Aubameyang began to build his career, securing a permanent contract with Saint-Étienne and scoring 35 league goals over two seasons from 2011.

## LONDON CALLING

In the January 2018 transfer window, Aubameyang swapped the Bundesliga for the Premier League in a club-record move to Arsenal. The switch went through on deadline day as Auba arrived at the Emirates in a £56-millon move. Reunited with Dortmund teammate Henrikh Mkhitaryan, the Gabon striker continued his goalscoring form with a first goal for the Gunners against Everton.

## BUNDESLIGA'S BEST

After a summer 2013 move to Borussia Dortmund, Aubameyang became the first player in the club's history to mark his league debut with a hat-trick. He scored more than 140 goals for the club over five seasons. Alongside his sharp shooting, another of his weapons is his speed – he could match 100m world-record holder Usain Bolt for at least 30m. In 2016–17, Aubameyang was the Bundesliga's top scorer ahead of Robert Lewandowski.

Aubameyang skippers Gabon and is the Panthers' record goalscorer with 23 goals.

**FOOTIE FACT**

***Aubameyang warmed-up for Saint-Étienne in 2012 wearing a pair of boots encrusted with crystals.***

# GARETH BALE

Bale began his career with Southampton as a fearless full-back and master of free-kicks. A £7-million move to Tottenham in 2007 saw him switch position and the **WELSH WIZARD** excelled as a winger. His attacking qualities took him to Real Madrid in 2013 for a then **WORLD-RECORD** transfer fee. Since joining *Los Blancos*, Bale hasn't looked back, winning La Liga and three UEFA Champions League titles.

**REAL MADRID**

**MIDFIELDER**

**FULL NAME:** Gareth Frank Bale
**NICKNAME:** The Cannon
**DATE OF BIRTH:** 16 July 1989
**PLACE OF BIRTH:** Cardiff, Wales
**HEIGHT:** 1.85m **WEIGHT:** 82kg
**LEFT OR RIGHT FOOTED:** Both
**SQUAD NUMBER:** 11
**INTERNATIONAL TEAM:** Wales

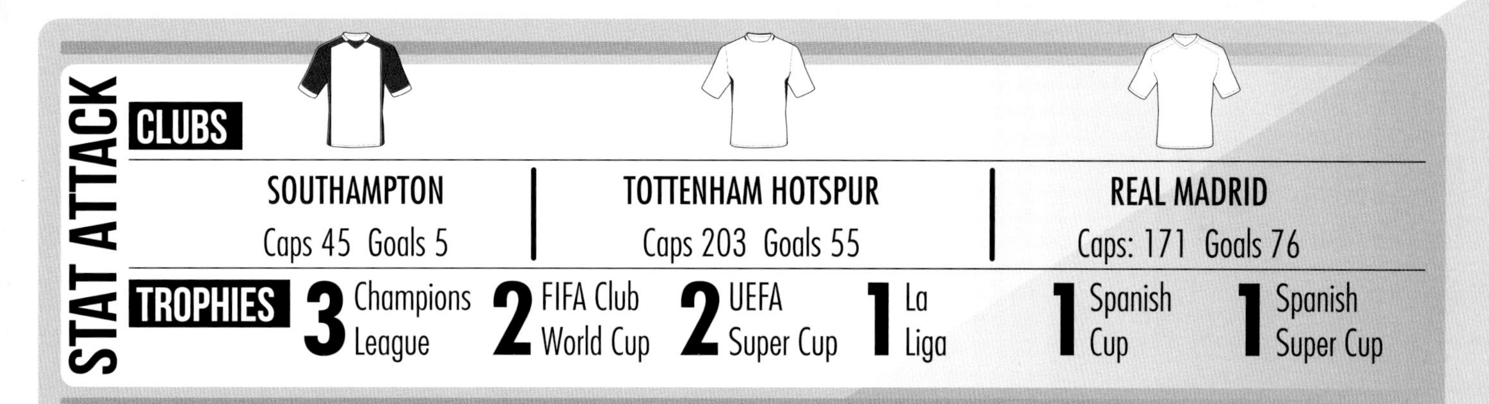

# STAT ATTACK

**CLUBS**

| SOUTHAMPTON | TOTTENHAM HOTSPUR | REAL MADRID |
| --- | --- | --- |
| Caps 45 Goals 5 | Caps 203 Goals 55 | Caps: 171 Goals 76 |

**TROPHIES**

- 3 Champions League
- 2 FIFA Club World Cup
- 2 UEFA Super Cup
- 1 La Liga
- 1 Spanish Cup
- 1 Spanish Super Cup

## TOP AT TOTTENHAM

Six seasons with Spurs saw Bale become an outstanding player. With the pace and acceleration of an Olympic sprinter, Bale operated first as a winger and later as a second striker, devastating defences with his deadly dribbling and powerful shots. A string of individual awards and impressive performances, including a hat-trick against Inter Milan in 2010, put Bale at the top of most clubs' wanted lists, and when Real Madrid came calling in 2013 the offer of around 100 million Euros sealed the deal.

## REAL DEAL

Over five seasons, Bale has been part of an awesome Real Madrid team that has won the Spanish League title, the Spanish Cup and three UEFA Champions Leagues. Madrid's performances are always better with Bale on the pitch and he has contributed over 70 goals and 50 assists for *Los Blancos*. Gareth's stats at Madrid would be better still had he not suffered so many injuries, mainly to his calves. Bale has scored more La Liga goals than any other British player, having smashed Gary Lineker's 42-goal record back in 2016, and he would love to end his career at the Bernabéu.

## WELSH DRAGON

At 16 years and 315 days, Bale became the (then) youngest player to feature for Wales and the youngest goalscorer soon after. Fifty caps later and he had helped his country qualify for their first major finals in almost 60 years. Some outstanding performances at EURO 2016, with three goals from Bale, saw Wales reach the semi-finals, losing to the eventual champions, Portugal. He now has over 25 international goals and is targeting Wales' all-time goalscoring record.

Bale helped Wales go all the way to the semi-finals of EURO 2016.

### FOOTIE FACT

***Bale's favourite squad number is 11, though he has worn 3, 37, 22 and 16 at different times in his career.***

# LEONARDO BONUCCI

A fabulous **ALL-ROUND DEFENDER**, Bonucci's best position is in the heart of a three-man defence. His strengths are solid tackling, great positional play and passes up the pitch. His rise to the top took some time – he has been on the books of six different Italian clubs – but at **JUVENTUS** he developed into a world-class stopper, winning 13 trophies including **SIX** League titles.

**DEFENDER**

**NICKNAME:** Bonnibauer
**DATE OF BIRTH:** 1 May 1987
**PLACE OF BIRTH:** Viterbo, Italy
**HEIGHT:** 1.90m **WEIGHT:** 82kg
**LEFT OR RIGHT FOOTED:** Right
**SQUAD NUMBER:** 19
**INTERNATIONAL TEAM:** Italy

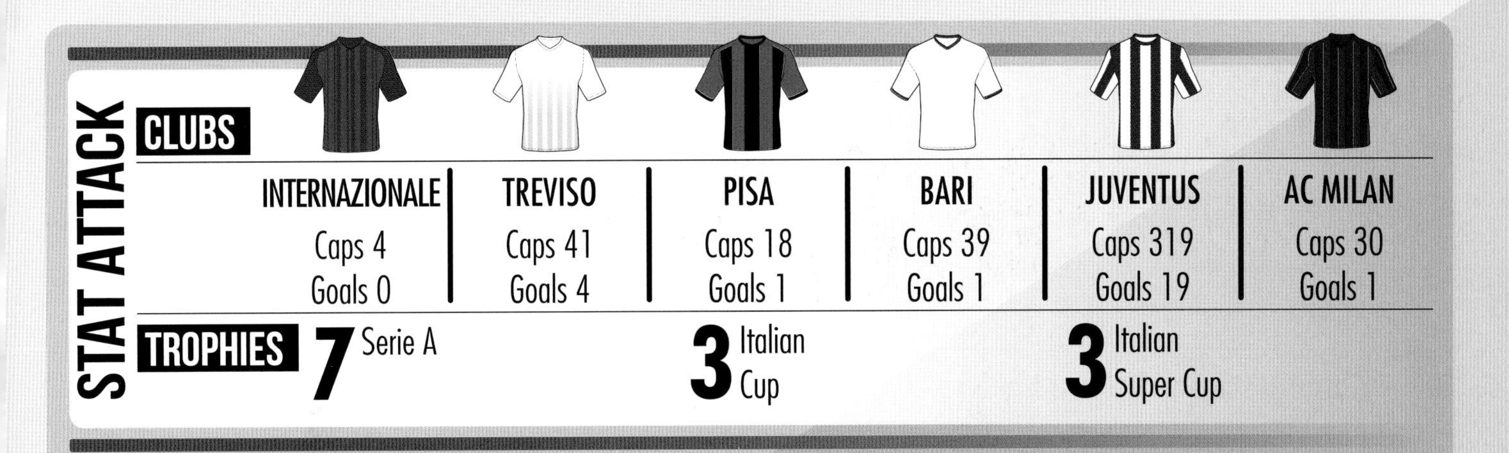

## STAT ATTACK

**CLUBS**

| INTERNAZIONALE | TREVISO | PISA | BARI | JUVENTUS | AC MILAN |
|---|---|---|---|---|---|
| Caps 4 | Caps 41 | Caps 18 | Caps 39 | Caps 319 | Caps 30 |
| Goals 0 | Goals 4 | Goals 1 | Goals 1 | Goals 19 | Goals 1 |

**TROPHIES**

| | |
|---|---|
| 7 | Serie A |
| 3 | Italian Cup |
| 3 | Italian Super Cup |

## GOLDEN YEARS

When Juventus bought Bonucci in the summer of 2010, it was the start of something special. He went straight into the side alongside Italy teammate Giorgio Chiellini. He and Chiellini later partnered with Andrea Barzagli, forming a trio at the back nicknamed 'BBC'. Six Italian league titles were won in a row, along with three Italian Cups. Bonucci also reached two UEFA Champions League finals, but was on the losing side both times, to Barcelona in 2015 and Real Madrid in 2017. In 2016 he was voted Italy's footballer of the year and named in the UEFA Team of the Year.

## MILAN MOVE

When Bonucci moved to Juve's rivals AC Milan in the summer of 2017, it was one of the most surprising transfers of recent seasons. He left a team that had twice finished runners-up in the UEFA Champions League to join a club that hadn't even qualified for that season's tournament. Milan paid £37.5 million for the 30-year-old and made him their captain. While Bonucci has had a rocky start at Milan so far, don't bet against this determined defender coming back even stronger.

Bonucci is a leader on the pitch for club and country.

## ITALY INTERNATIONAL

With 75 caps and five goals for his country, Bonucci's international career has had many highs and lows. He was first called up to play for Italy in March 2010 and made the World Cup squad, but was an unused substitute as they were knocked out in the first round. Two years later it was a different story – Bonucci started in all but one match as Italy reached the final of EURO 2012, losing 4–0 to Spain. Another miserable World Cup followed in 2014, though Bonucci was made captain following the tournament. Sadly for the defender, Italy did not qualify for the 2018 World Cup, losing in a play-off match to Sweden.

## FOOTIE FACT

***Bonucci broke his nose after only 30 seconds in Italy's World Cup play-off match against Sweden in 2017. Incredibly, he managed to play on for the entire match!***

# THIBAUT COURTOIS

Belgian Courtois joined Genk at the age of seven and was made **FIRST-CHOICE** goalkeeper for the club aged just 16. In 2010–11 he kept 14 clean sheets to help Genk in their title win in the Belgian Pro League. A **GIANT** of a shot-stopper, Courtois is a commanding figure in his penalty area. He's already been champion in **THREE** different countries and still has the best years of his career ahead of him.

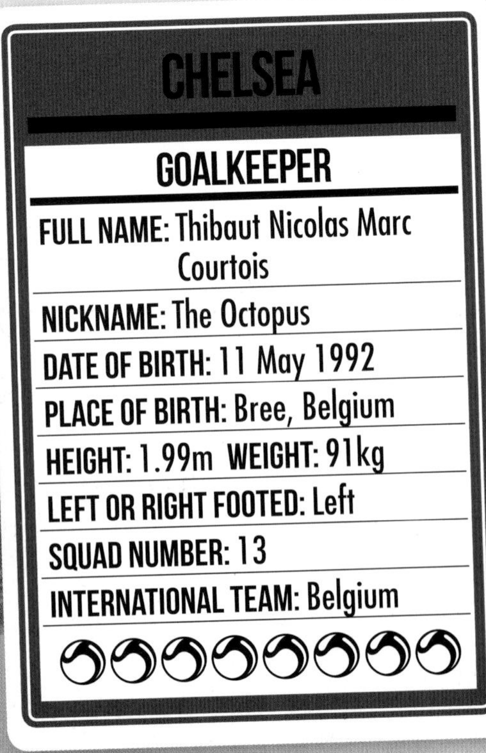
CHELSEA

GOALKEEPER

**FULL NAME:** Thibaut Nicolas Marc Courtois

**NICKNAME:** The Octopus

**DATE OF BIRTH:** 11 May 1992

**PLACE OF BIRTH:** Bree, Belgium

**HEIGHT:** 1.99m **WEIGHT:** 91kg

**LEFT OR RIGHT FOOTED:** Left

**SQUAD NUMBER:** 13

**INTERNATIONAL TEAM:** Belgium

STAT ATTACK

**CLUBS**

| GENK | ATLÉTICO MADRID (LOAN) | CHELSEA |
|---|---|---|
| Caps 45 Goals 0 | Caps 154 Goals 0 | Caps 142 Goals 0 |

**TROPHIES**

| Number | Trophy |
|---|---|
| 1 | Belgian Pro League |
| 1 | La Liga |
| 1 | Spanish Cup |
| 1 | UEFA Europa League |
| 1 | UEFA Super Cup |
| 2 | Premier League |
| 1 | League Cup |

# ATLÉTICO EDUCATION

Courtois joined Atlético Madrid on loan in 2011, only weeks after arriving at Chelsea from Genk for £7 million. Over three seasons, he helped Atlético to win La Liga, the UEFA Europa League, the UEFA Super Cup and the Spanish Cup. He came very close to winning the UEFA Champions League too, but lost in the final in 2014 after Real Madrid equalized in the last minute of normal time. When he returned to parent club Chelsea aged 22, Courtois was regarded as the world's best young goalkeeper and had a Ballon d'Or nomination under his belt.

# CHELSEA CHAMPION

Only a very special keeper could replace the legendary Petr Cech between the sticks, and that's exactly what Courtois did on his return to Chelsea. Since making his debut for the Blues, Thibaut has shone individually and added the League Cup and two Premier League titles to his trophy collection – and he's still only in his mid-twenties! His 16 clean sheets in the 2016–17 campaign ensured he ended the season with the Premier League Golden Glove award. A superb shot-stopper with a champion's character, Chelsea will be keen to extend Courtois' contract.

# BRILLIANT BELGIUM

Courtois is part of Belgium's 'golden generation'. This talented group of players, skippered by Thibaut's Chelsea team-mate Eden Hazard, reached the quarter-finals of the World Cup in 2014 in Brazil and again at EURO 2016. Belgium even topped the FIFA World Rankings for the first time in November 2015. Courtois has been key to the side's success and is passionate about keeping his top spot for the national team. Look out for some strong performances in the future.

Courtois has over 50 caps for his country and is the youngest goalkeeper to play for Belgium.

## FOOTIE FACT

***While the other Atlético players drove flash supercars to training, 19-year-old Courtois used to arrive by bike! That is until his prankster team-mates took his bike apart...***

# PHILIPPE COUTINHO

Creative Coutinho joined Liverpool in January 2013.

He stood out as one of the Premier League's **TOP PERFORMERS** during his five years with the Reds. His touch, vision and stunning **CREATIVE PLAY** saw him quickly become an Anfield favourite. A dream move to Barcelona in January 2018 for a fee of up to **£142 MILLION** saw him team up with Lionel Messi and Luis Suárez.

BARCELONA

**ATTACKING MIDFIELDER**

**FULL NAME:** Philippe Coutinho Correia

**NICKNAMES:** The Little Magician, The Kid

**DATE OF BIRTH:** 12 June 1992

**PLACE OF BIRTH:** Rio de Janeiro, Brazil

**HEIGHT:** 1.71m **WEIGHT:** 68kg

**LEFT OR RIGHT FOOTED:** Both

**SQUAD NUMBER:** 14

**INTERNATIONAL TEAM:** Brazil

## STAT ATTACK

**CLUBS**

| VASCO DA GAMA (LOAN) | INTERNAZIONALE | ESPANYOL (LOAN) | LIVERPOOL | BARCELONA |
|---|---|---|---|---|
| Caps 43 Goals 5 | Caps 47 Goals 5 | Caps 16 Goals 5 | Caps 201 Goals 54 | Caps 6 Goals 1 |

**TROPHIES** 1 Italian Super Cup 1 Italian Cup

**RUSSIA 2018 WAS COUTINHO'S FIRST WORLD CUP TOURNAMENT.**

# CLUB CAREER

Like so many young Brazilians, Coutinho grew up playing futsal, a game played on a hard surface where technical skill is king. He joined Vasco da Gama's youth academy and rose through the ranks. Italian superclub Inter Milan paid £2.25 million for him in 2008, but agreed that Coutinho could stay at Vasco on loan for two years. When he was 18, Coutinho finally moved to Inter but could not hold down a regular first-team place. Another loan move to Spain came in January 2012 as Coutinho hit fantastic form with Espanyol.

# KING OF THE KOP

Coutinho joined Liverpool in January 2013 for a fee of £8.5 million – a snip considering he is now worth well over £100 million! He reached double figures for goals and assists in every full season for the Reds and was regularly at the heart of their attacks. The Brazil international was also Liverpool's Player of the Season two years running. Barcelona targeted the attacking midfielder in summer 2017, and eventually got their man in January 2018 for a staggering £142 million. Coutinho opened his account for Barça by scoring in the Spanish Cup semi-final win at Valencia.

# BRAZILIAN BOY

Coutinho's first senior appearance for Brazil came in October 2010, although he didn't become a regular for the national side until 2015. He was left out of the squad for the 2014 FIFA World Cup in his home country, but now he regularly stars alongside Neymar and co. His goals helped Brazil qualify for the 2018 World Cup in Russia but he needs to stay fully fit to compete at the highest level.

Coutinho is often compared to fellow countryman Ronaldinho, the legendary playmaker.

## FOOTIE FACT

**Growing up, Coutinho used to play as Steven Gerrard on his PlayStation. It was his dream come true to actually play alongside his idol at Liverpool!**

# KEVIN DE BRUYNE

In Manchester City, **MIDFIELD MAESTRO** Kevin de Bruyne has finally found a club to call home. He was signed for a reported fee of £54.5 million in August 2015 and has been in **STUNNING FORM** ever since. 2017 saw him nominated for the prized **BALLON D'OR** award for the third year in a row.

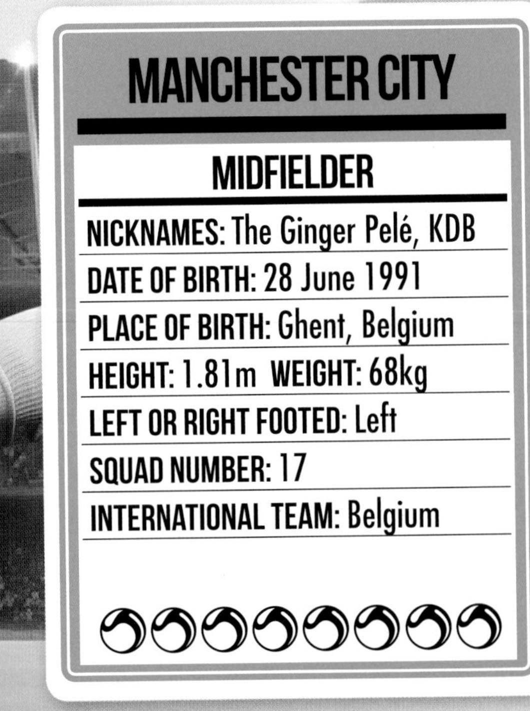

## MANCHESTER CITY

### MIDFIELDER

**NICKNAMES:** The Ginger Pelé, KDB
**DATE OF BIRTH:** 28 June 1991
**PLACE OF BIRTH:** Ghent, Belgium
**HEIGHT:** 1.81m **WEIGHT:** 68kg
**LEFT OR RIGHT FOOTED:** Left
**SQUAD NUMBER:** 17
**INTERNATIONAL TEAM:** Belgium

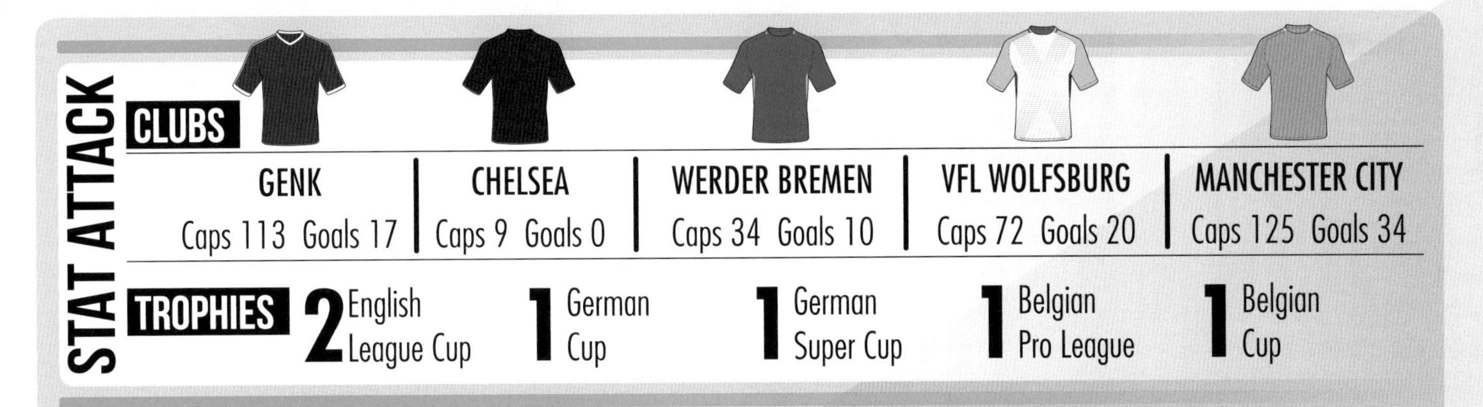

## STAT ATTACK

| CLUBS | GENK | CHELSEA | WERDER BREMEN | VFL WOLFSBURG | MANCHESTER CITY |
|---|---|---|---|---|---|
| | Caps 113 Goals 17 | Caps 9 Goals 0 | Caps 34 Goals 10 | Caps 72 Goals 20 | Caps 125 Goals 34 |
| TROPHIES | 2 English League Cup | 1 German Cup | 1 German Super Cup | 1 Belgian Pro League | 1 Belgian Cup |

# GROWING UP

Kevin de Bruyne's childhood had an international flavour – his mother was born in Burundi, his father is Belgian and he travelled regularly between England and Africa. De Bruyne eventually settled on Belgium as his national team. His first senior appearance was for Belgian club Genk in 2009, where he played a key role in the club's title-winning side, making 17 assists and scoring six goals from the heart of midfield. A move to London followed in January 2012 when Chelsea signed de Bruyne, but loaned him straight back to Genk.

# GERMAN GIANT

At the start of the 2012–13 season de Bruyne switched to the Bundesliga, joining German club Werder Bremen on a season-long loan. After a successful campaign, he returned to parent club Chelsea, but could not get into the first team. Desperate for game time, de Bruyne signed for Wolfsburg in an £18-million permanent move. He made a huge impact, providing a record-breaking number of assists for the club as Wolfsburg finished as runners-up in the league and as German Cup winners. It was only a matter of time before a bigger club came calling for Germany's Footballer of the Year in 2015.

# CITY SLICKER

De Bruyne joined Manchester City in August 2015 for a club-record fee, and has been a standout performer in City's first XI, contributing 34 goals and over 50 assists in his first 125 appearances in all competitions. Kevin has confessed that he actually prefers to create goals for his team-mates rather than score them! Along with his creativity and defence-splitting passes, de Bruyne's reputation for hard work saw him quickly become a crowd favourite. He is now playing the best football of his career and is a key man for the free-scoring Sky Blues.

De Bruyne cemented his place as a regular for Belgium during the 2018 FIFA World Cup qualifiers.

## FOOTIE FACT

***As befits a player with an international childhood, Kevin is fluent in Dutch, French and English.***

# ANTOINE GRIEZMANN

Griezmann is quite simply a brilliant **ATTACKING** player who has earned his place among football's **ELITE**. Europe's top clubs have repeatedly been linked with a bid for Griezmann, who is worth around £130 million thanks to his **MAGNIFICENT** goals and desire to win, so he may be on the move before long. Until then, Griezmann will continue to perform for Atlético Madrid, and as a key man for France.

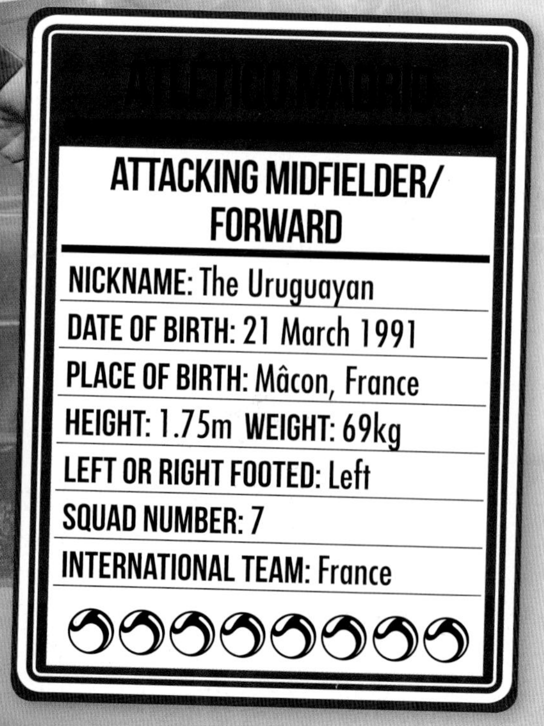

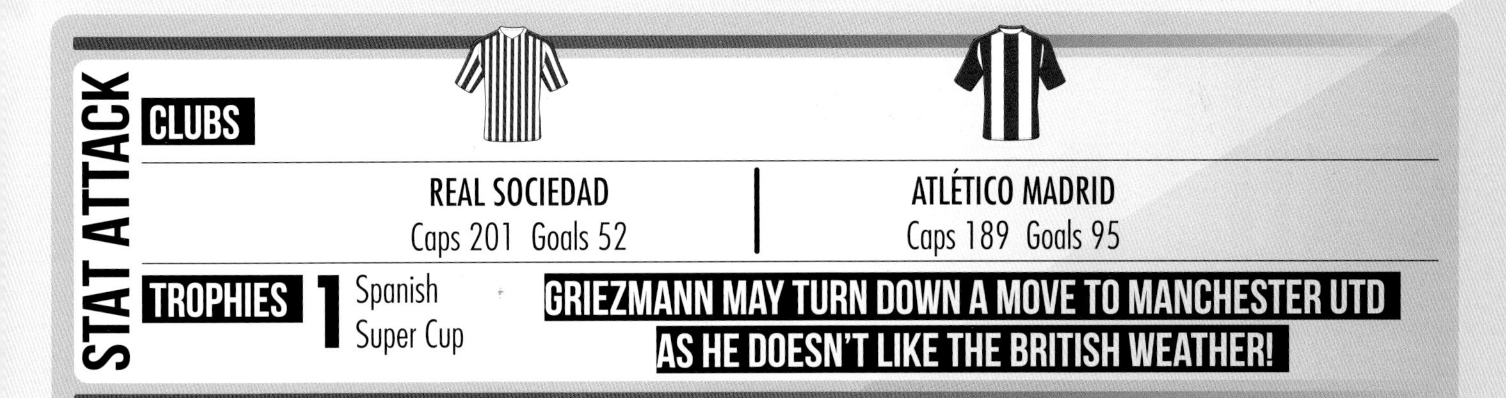

## STAT ATTACK

**CLUBS**

| REAL SOCIEDAD | ATLÉTICO MADRID |
| --- | --- |
| Caps 201 Goals 52 | Caps 189 Goals 95 |

**TROPHIES** 1 Spanish Super Cup

**GRIEZMANN MAY TURN DOWN A MOVE TO MANCHESTER UTD AS HE DOESN'T LIKE THE BRITISH WEATHER!**

## SHORT STORY

Growing up, Griezmann was rejected by more than one French club for being too short and skinny. Determined to prove them wrong, a 14-year-old Griezmann was picked up on trial by Spanish club Real Sociedad, who offered him a youth contract. After four years, he skipped the reserves and made his first-team debut in September 2009. Griezmann went on to make over 200 appearances for the club that had showed such faith in him, turning down reported interest from Lyon, Manchester United and Arsenal to remain with Real. It was a period when Griezmann's reputation as a technically gifted team player grew.

## FRENCH FLAIR

Griezmann has a German-sounding surname as his father comes from the Alsace region of France that borders Germany. He was not on the radar of France's international coaches at youth level as he was playing his football in Spain, and didn't link up with his national side until he was 19. A senior call-up came in February 2014 and Griezmann joined the France squad for the 2014 World Cup that summer. France were knocked out in the quarter-finals by eventual champions Germany, but Griezmann enjoyed a stunning EURO 2016, claiming the Golden Boot with six goals and two assists in seven games, and was also named the tournament's best player.

## MADRID'S MAIN MAN

In 2014, Real sold Griezmann to Atlético Madrid for a cool £24 million. He quickly settled into the team with a string of goals and match-winning performances, finishing his first season at Atlético with 22 league goals in 37 games. The following season saw Griezmann contribute important UEFA Champions League goals, only for the club to lose in the final to local rivals Real Madrid in an agonisingly close penalty shoot-out. In the summer of 2017, Griezmann rejected a blockbuster move to Manchester United, choosing to stay at Atlético and help them through their transfer ban. Griezmann loves the responsibility of being Atlético's main man.

Unlike most footballers, Griezmann does not have an agent.

### FOOTIE FACT

***Griezmann wears long-sleeved shirts and the number 7 in honour of his idol, David Beckham.***

# EDEN HAZARD

Chelsea's **BELGIAN ACE** in midfield, Hazard has flair and pace. His six seasons at Stamford Bridge have seen him mature into one of the finest players in the world, often compared to Messi and Ronaldo. A **SUPERB PASSER**, Hazard can operate on either wing or in central midfield, thanks to his skill with **BOTH FEET**. He's claimed three league titles, and the UEFA Champions League and the Ballon d'Or are his next goals.

**CHELSEA**

**ATTACKING MIDFIELDER**

**FULL NAME:** Eden Michael Hazard
**NICKNAME:** N/A
**DATE OF BIRTH:** 7 January 1991
**PLACE OF BIRTH:** La Louvière, Belgium
**HEIGHT:** 1.73m **WEIGHT:** 76kg
**LEFT OR RIGHT FOOTED:** Both
**SQUAD NUMBER:** 10
**INTERNATIONAL TEAM:** Belgium

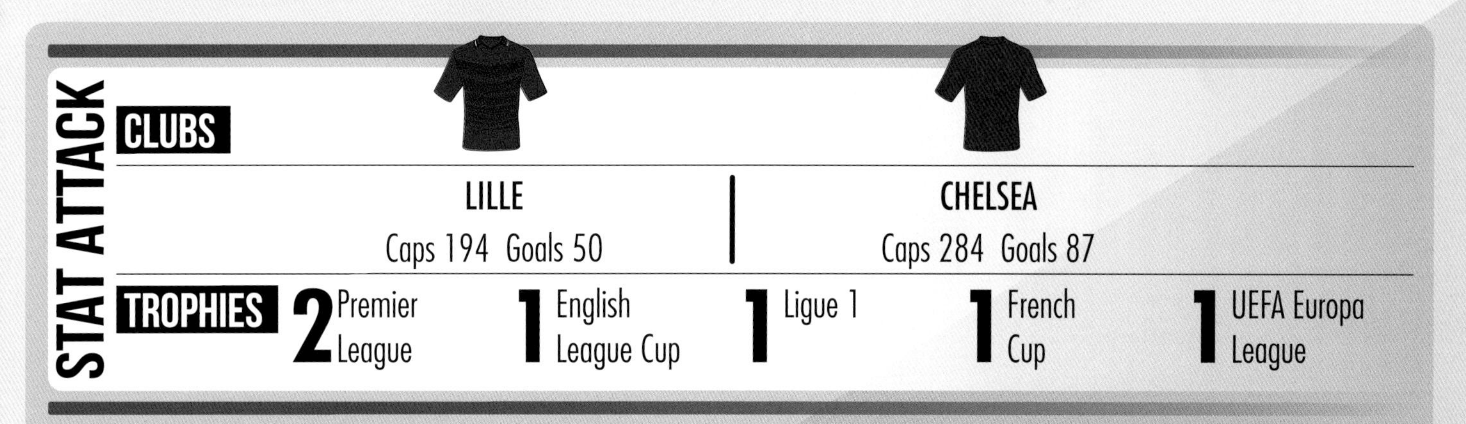


## FRENCH CONNECTION

Hazard joined French Ligue 1 club Lille's academy at the age of 14. The young star became a permanent member of the first team soon after making his pro debut, aged just 16, and quickly made a big impact in midfield. He was named France's Young Player of the Year twice in a row, in 2009 and 2010, becoming the first non-French player to win the award. Fast and technically gifted, Hazard played almost 200 times for Lille, scoring 50 goals. His finest season was in 2010–11, when Lille won a league and cup double.

## HERO HAZARD

With the world at his feet, Hazard signed for Chelsea aged 21 for a fee of £32 million in the summer of 2012. His first season ended with him scoring 13 goals in all competitions. With some first-class performances under José Mourinho, by May 2015 Hazard had been voted Chelsea's Player of the Year two seasons running as the Blues ran away with the Premier League title and won the League Cup. In 2016–17 Chelsea were crowned champions and Hazard was the hero once again.

## YOUNG SKIPPER

Hazard won his first cap for Belgium aged 17, but had to wait three years to score his first international goal. He has since played over 80 times for the Red Devils, and scored over 20 goals. Belgium's star-studded golden generation reached the quarter-finals of both the 2014 World Cup and EURO 2016. With Hazard wearing the captain's armband, Belgium are an organized and dangerous side.

Thanks to his years at Lille, Hazard was eligible to play for France, but he chose his home country instead.

## FOOTIE FACT

***Belgium once banned Hazard for three matches after he left a EURO 2012 qualifier early to go for a burger after having being subbed. Now he follows a much healthier diet!***

# ANDRÉS INIESTA

The **MAGICAL MIDFIELDER** has won every honour in the game, including eight Spanish league titles and four UEFA Champions Leagues. Iniesta was the **DRIVING FORCE** behind Spain's recent dominance in international football, winning the EUROs twice and the **WORLD CUP** in 2010. He is probably the **BEST PLAYER** never to have won the Ballon d'Or.

BARCELONA

**FORWARD**

**FULL NAME:** Andrés Iniesta Luján

**NICKNAMES:** El Ilusionista (The Illusionist), El Cerebro (The Brain)

**DATE OF BIRTH:** 11 May 1984

**PLACE OF BIRTH:** Fuentealbilla, Spain

**HEIGHT:** 1.71m **WEIGHT:** 68kg

**LEFT OR RIGHT FOOTED:** Both

**SQUAD NUMBER:** 8

**INTERNATIONAL TEAM:** Spain

## LEAVING HOME

Iniesta was just 10 years old and playing for his local club Albacete's youth team when he caught the eye of the Barcelona scouts. He was invited to join Barça's famous La Masia academy aged 12, and left his family and village to follow his dream. A shy boy, Iniesta had to overcome homesickness, but by the age of 15, he was made Barcelona's U15 captain and was showing skills beyond his years. The then first-team captain Pep Guardiola predicted that the young Iniesta would take his position one day – and he was right!

## ONE-CLUB MAN

Iniesta made his first-team debut for Barcelona in October 2002, the first of more than an incredible 650 appearances for the club so far. His trophy cabinet is pretty special – he's won an impressive eight La Liga titles and the UEFA Champions League four times. Iniesta has captained the side since 2015 and shares the club record of winning 30 trophies with Lionel Messi. He has signed a lifetime contract with the La Liga giants and intends to finish his career with the club.

## SPARKLING SPANIARD

Iniesta was a key man as Spain sparkled between 2008 and 2012, twice winning the European Championship and the World Cup in 2010. Iniesta scored the extra-time winner in the 2010 World Cup final against the Netherlands to clinch the trophy for the first time in Spain's history. His exceptional creative passing and goals also saw him named Player of the Tournament at EURO 2012. Iniesta joined Spain's 100-cap club at the 2014 World Cup.

Andrés Iniesta – one of Spain's greatest-ever players.

## FOOTIE FACT

***Iniesta is a co-owner of Albacete Balompié, his old youth team, and also owns a vineyard in the village where he grew up.***

# ISCO

Real Madrid and Spain's **PLAYMAKER**

Francisco Suárez is more commonly known as Isco. The creative midfielder is currently playing the best football of his career under Zinedine Zidane, growing in **CONFIDENCE** and in reputation with each season he plays at the Bernabéu. He was shortlisted for the 2017 Ballon d'Or prize and is already into **DOUBLE FIGURES** for major trophies.

**REAL MADRID**

**ATTACKING MIDFIELDER**

**FULL NAME:** Francisco Román Alarcón Suárez

**NICKNAME:** Maggia (Magic)

**DATE OF BIRTH:** 21 April 1992

**PLACE OF BIRTH:** Benalmádena, Spain

**HEIGHT:** 1.76m **WEIGHT:** 79kg

**LEFT OR RIGHT FOOTED:** Right

**SQUAD NUMBER:** 22

**INTERNATIONAL TEAM:** Spain

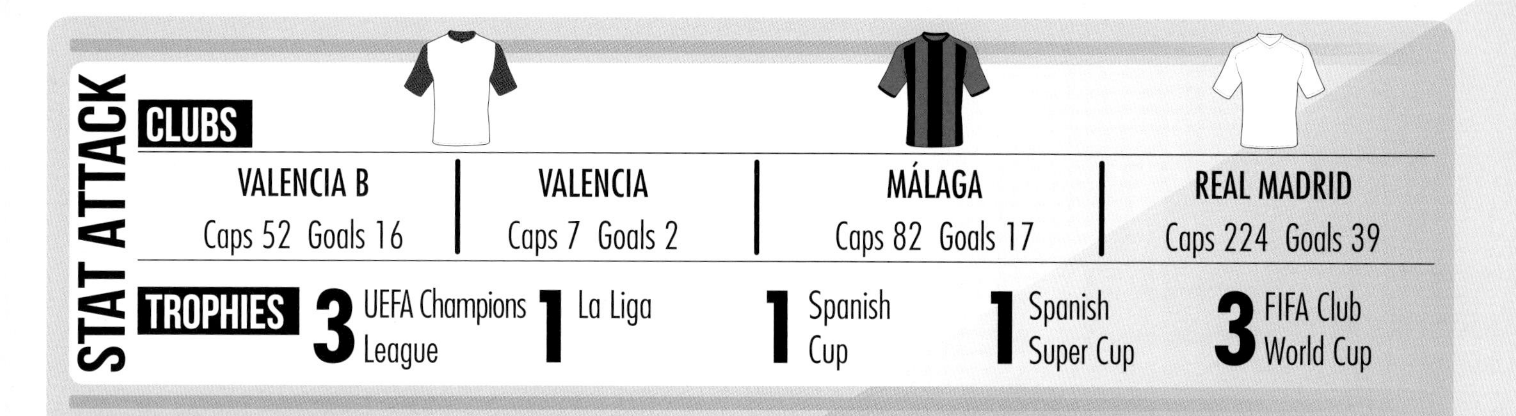

STAT ATTACK

**CLUBS**

| VALENCIA B | VALENCIA | MÁLAGA | REAL MADRID |
|---|---|---|---|
| Caps 52 Goals 16 | Caps 7 Goals 2 | Caps 82 Goals 17 | Caps 224 Goals 39 |

**TROPHIES**

| 3 | 1 | 1 | 1 | 3 |
|---|---|---|---|---|
| UEFA Champions League | La Liga | Spanish Cup | Spanish Super Cup | FIFA Club World Cup |

## FALSE START

Francisco Román Alarcón Suárez was born in Benalmádena, a town outside Málaga that's better known for its beaches than its football. A few clubs showed interest in him as a very young teenager, but the 14-year-old Isco chose to move 600km away and join Valencia, who had recently won two league titles. Despite his pace, skill on the ball and precision passing, Isco played only seven games for Valencia's first team. A spell in the B team saw him score 16 goals, and Isco knew he had to move on if he was to fulfil his potential.

## MAKING HISTORY

Málaga came in for Isco after meeting the £4.5-million buy-out clause in his Valencia contract, and the promise of first-team football at a club close to home was too good for him to turn down. The Valencia fans were not happy, especially as Isco had been allowed to leave for such a small fee. In his second season with Málaga, Isco turned in some top performances as the club competed in the UEFA Champions League for the first time and reached the quarter-finals. They also finished sixth in the league, with Isco contributing 12 goals and four assists that season.

## REAL REGULAR

As Isco won the Golden Boy award in 2012, Real Madrid saw the young playmaker's potential. He was now a regular in Spain's brilliant Under-21 side. In June 2013, Real paid a reported £23 million to bring Isco to the Bernabéu. Many of his 11 goals in 53 games in his first season came from the subs bench, but Isco played for most of the 2014 UEFA Champions League final, a 4–1 victory over Madrid rivals Atlético. Real had won the Spanish Cup a month earlier and Isco has since added several more major trophies to his collection, including the league title and another two UEFA Champions League crowns in 2016 and 2017. Now he's one of the first names on Real's team sheet.

Isco made his debut for Spain in February 2013 after impressing in the youth teams.

**FOOTIE FACT**

***Isco is a lifelong Barcelona fan and has a dog called Messi. His idol growing up was Spain team-mate Andrés Iniesta.***

# HARRY KANE

Harry Kane has developed into a **SUPERSTAR STRIKER**, with a lethal touch in front of goal and an excellent scoring record. When Kane gets on a hot streak there's almost no defence that can stop him! His **SUPERB FINISHING** ability, brilliant hold-up play and close control mean he can also play as a lone striker. He's a **TRULY GREAT** goalscorer.

## TOTTENHAM HOTSPUR

### FORWARD

**FULL NAME:** Harry Edward Kane
**NICKNAME:** The Hurrikane
**DATE OF BIRTH:** 28 July 1993
**PLACE OF BIRTH:** London, England
**HEIGHT:** 1.88m **WEIGHT:** 86kg
**LEFT OR RIGHT FOOTED:** Right
**SQUAD NUMBER:** 10
**INTERNATIONAL TEAM:** England

STAT ATTACK

CLUBS

| LEYTON ORIENT (LOAN) | MILLWALL (LOAN) | NORWICH CITY (LOAN) | LEICESTER CITY (LOAN) | TOTTENHAM HOTSPUR |
|---|---|---|---|---|
| Caps 18 Goals 5 | Caps 27 Goals 9 | Caps 5 Goals 0 | Caps 15 Goals 2 | Caps 199 Goals 132 |

**KANE SCORED 56 GOALS FOR CLUB AND COUNTRY IN 2017 – MORE THAN ANY OTHER PLAYER IN EUROPE'S TOP FIVE LEAGUES.**

## SHARP SHOOTER

Kane joined Tottenham aged 11. His breakthrough came in 2014–15 when he smashed home 21 goals in 34 league games for Spurs. The following season Harry claimed his first Premier League Golden Boot with 25 league goals from 38 top-flight appearances. Despite missing 11 weeks of the 2016–17 season through injury, Kane hit another 29 league goals from just 30 games to win his second Golden Boot. He has his eye on Alan Shearer's all-time Premier League goal record of 260 and, still in his mid-twenties, he has time on his side in the battle of the goal-kings.

## LOAN RANGER

In a bid to kickstart his career, Spurs loaned Kane out to Leyton Orient, Millwall, Norwich and Leicester, but he never made a major impact at any of his loan clubs. Some critics claimed that Kane was not cut out to play at the highest level, but he worked hard to prove them wrong. An old-fashioned number 10, Kane has a real passion for the game and loves nothing better than scoring goals. Harry improved his strength and physique to earn his first start under manager Mauricio Pochettino. The rest is history!

## LEADING THE LINE

Kane is England's main man up front. With an international scoring record of a goal every two matches, Kane will be keen to add to his tally as he continues playing for England. Kane made his England debut in March 2015 and was part of the squad for EURO 2016. When he captained the side for the first time in a World Cup qualifier against Scotland, it was a boyhood dream come true for Harry.

Kane has made over 20 appearances for his country and is an England regular.

## FOOTIE FACT

***Kane was once a member of Arsenal's youth academy, but was let go by the Gunners after only one season.***

# N'GOLO KANTÉ

Back-to-back Premier League glory with Leicester City and Chelsea has seen Kanté go from **ZERO TO HERO** in just two years. He's now become one of the **WORLD'S FINEST** box-to-box midfielders, possessing a great passing range and with some **TERRIFIC TACKLES** in his locker.

**CHELSEA F.C.**

**MIDFIELDER**

**NICKNAME:** The Rat

**DATE OF BIRTH:** 29 March 1991

**PLACE OF BIRTH:** Paris, France

**HEIGHT:** 1.68m **WEIGHT:** 68kg

**LEFT OR RIGHT FOOTED:** Right

**SQUAD NUMBER:** 7

**INTERNATIONAL TEAM:** France

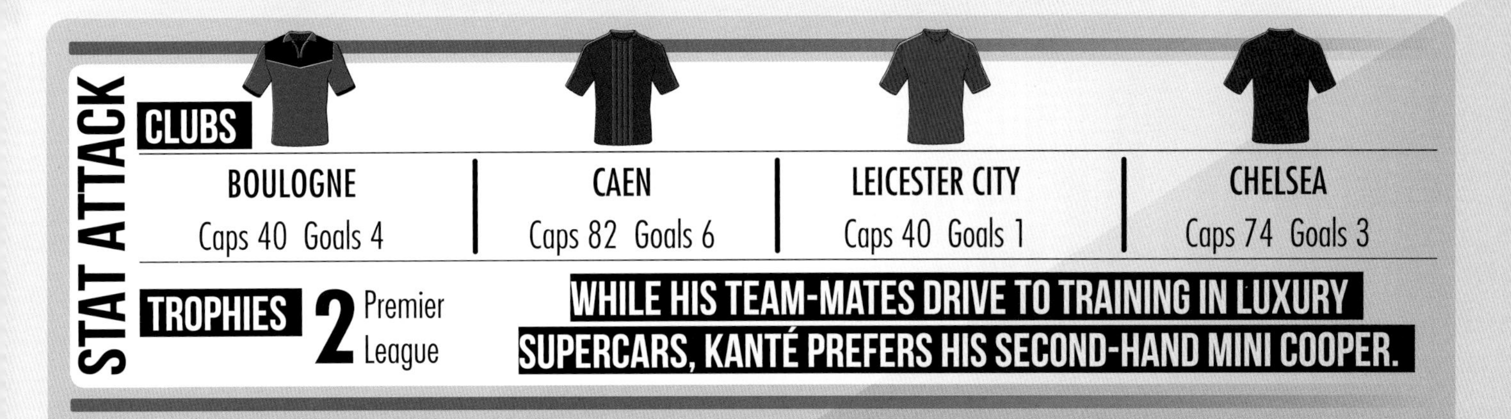


## CLIMBING THE LADDER

Kanté started out with youth team JS Suresnes in his home city of Paris, playing there until he was 18. He slipped through the nets of the scouts from the big clubs, as he was thought to be too short and not selfish enough on the ball. In 2010, he joined Boulogne and made his pro debut in the last game of the 2011–12 Ligue 2 season. He moved to Caen in 2013 and began to develop as a player. The following season he played 37 times for the club, newly promoted to Ligue 1, and made more tackles and interceptions than any other player in Europe that season.

## DREAM COME TRUE

To be given the number 7 shirt at such a famous club as Chelsea was Kanté's dream come true. He shone in his first season with the Blues, winning the Premier League trophy for the second year in a row. His solid form saw him pick up three individual awards – the PFA Player of the Year, FWA Player of the Year and the Premier League Player of the Season. A Ballon d'Or nomination topped off a fantastic season for the dynamic midfielder. His second campaign at Stamford Bridge saw Kanté continue his stunning form, with the UEFA Champions League the next title in the midfielder's sights.

Many football experts consider N'Golo Kanté to be France's best player.

## LEICESTER LEGEND

Kanté was the first player that Claudio Ranieri brought to Leicester City. When the midfielder signed from Caen for just £5.6 million, it turned out to be one of the transfers of the century, as Kanté helped lead the Foxes to a shock Premier League title. His displays as Leicester's engine in midfield brought him to the attention of Europe's biggest clubs and he was snapped up by Chelsea for £32 million in the summer of 2016. Once Kanté had moved on, the Foxes' form went seriously downhill – Leicester's loss was certainly Chelsea's gain.

### FOOTIE FACT

**Kanté is one of nine children and has four brothers and four sisters. They grew up together in Paris.**

# TONI KROOS

A smart and **TECHNICALLY GIFTED** midfielder, Kroos has been with Real Madrid for four years. He joined *Los Blancos* fresh from winning the World Cup with Germany in 2014 and is respected for his ability to play in any midfield position and deliver **PERFECT PASSES**.

His list of honours speaks for itself – Kroos had collected over 20 **MAJOR TROPHIES** by the age of 27.

## REAL MADRID

### MIDFIELDER

**NICKNAME:** Garçom (The Waiter)

**DATE OF BIRTH:** 4 January 1990

**PLACE OF BIRTH:** Griefswald, Germany

**HEIGHT:** 1.83m **WEIGHT:** 76kg

**LEFT OR RIGHT FOOTED:** Both

**SQUAD NUMBER:** 8

**INTERNATIONAL TEAM:** Germany

STAT ATTACK

CLUBS

| BAYERN MUNICH II | BAYERN MUNICH | BAYER LEVERKUSEN (LOAN) | REAL MADRID |
| --- | --- | --- | --- |
| Caps 13 Goals 4 | Caps 205 Goals 25 | Caps 48 Goals 10 | Caps 176 Goals 11 |

TROPHIES

| | | | | |
| --- | --- | --- | --- | --- |
| 3 UEFA Champions League | 3 German Cup | 1 La Liga | 3 FIFA Club World Cup | 1 FIFA World Cup |
| 3 Bundesliga | 1 German Super Cup | 1 Spanish Super Cup | 4 UEFA Super Cup | |

# KROOS CONTROL

Kroos was called up to Bayern's first-team squad aged 17. At the time of his debut, he was the youngest player ever to represent Bayern in a pro match. A successful loan spell at Bayer Leverkusen from 2009 to 2010 saw Kroos play 48 matches for the side. He ended his time there with ten goals and a strong assists record. On his return to Munich in summer 2010, Kroos quickly became a first-team regular, winning three Bundesliga titles and a UEFA Champions League medal in 2013, although injury ruled him out of the final. His accurate passing and set-piece play gives Kroos the ability to control matches from midfield.

# WORLD CUP WONDER

In 2010, aged 20, Kroos broke into Germany's senior squad. He made the World Cup squad that year, as Germany reached the semi-finals in South Africa, but it was at the 2014 World Cup in Brazil that Kroos really raised his game. His man-of-the-match performances, two goals and four assists helped Germany win the World Cup for a fourth time. Kroos was unlucky to miss out on the Golden Ball for the best player of the tournament, which went to Lionel Messi. Some experts believe that Kroos is Germany's most important player.

# GERMAN GALÁCTICO

Kroos went in search of more silverware following his sparkling World Cup displays in a move to Real Madrid. *Los Blancos* paid a fee of £20–25 million in the summer of 2014. While he didn't light up the Bernabéu in his first couple of seasons, Kroos has found his best form since – he's known as a masterful midfielder with a pinpoint passing range. Toni has won the UEFA Champions League twice and the Spanish league title once with Real. He is the only German player to lift the Champions League trophy with two different clubs.

**Kroos in action in an international friendly against France, in November 2017.**

## FOOTIE FACT

***Kroos is the first footballer born in the former East Germany to have won the World Cup.***

# ROBERT LEWANDOWSKI

A **FANTASTIC FINISHER**, Bayern Munich's star striker is also captain of Poland. He is hailed as Poland's **GREATEST PLAYER** of all time, thanks to his glorious goal record, work-rate and leadership on the pitch. He **EXPLODED** on to the scene and scored 100 German top-flight goals faster than any player from outside Germany. It's no wonder he's valued at a cool £95 million!

BAYERN MUNICH

FORWARD

NICKNAME: The Body
DATE OF BIRTH: 21 August 1988
PLACE OF BIRTH: Warsaw, Poland
HEIGHT: 1.85m WEIGHT: 79kg
LEFT OR RIGHT FOOTED: Right
SQUAD NUMBER: 9
INTERNATIONAL TEAM: Poland

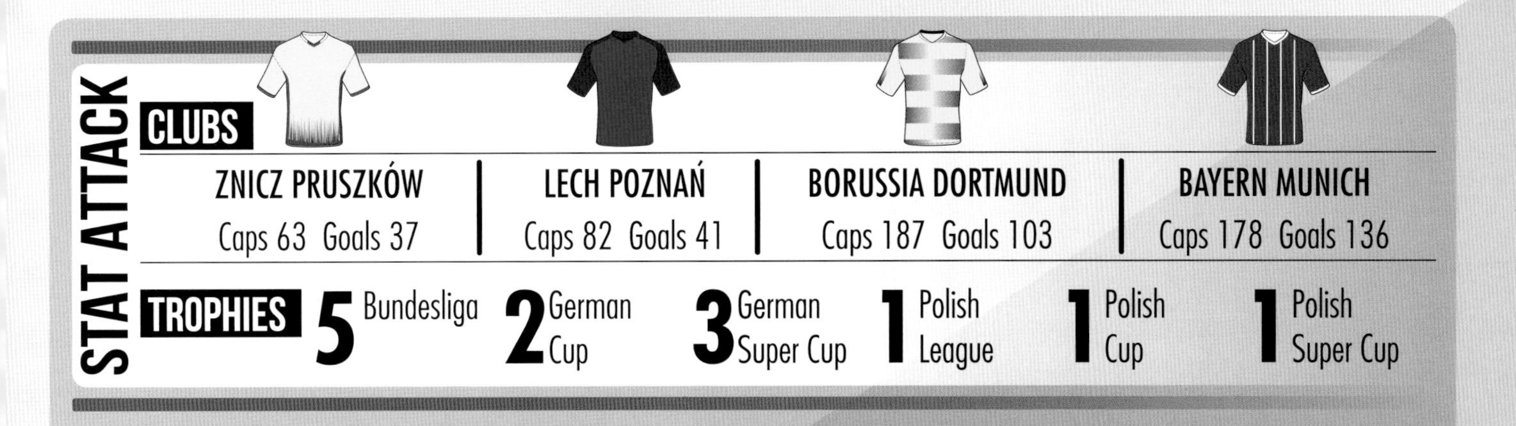


## A TASTE FOR GOAL

Robert kicked off his club career with Znicz Pruszków in the Polish third division. His 15 goals helped Znicz win promotion and the following season Lewandowski scored 21 goals in the second tier. In June 2008, the striker switched sides to top-flight side Lech Poznań, scoring on his debut. He was the league's top scorer in 2009–10 with 18 goals and led Lech to the title. His goalscoring form while playing in Poland was red-hot, earning Lewandowski a transfer to German club Borussia Dortmund in the summer of 2010. The move didn't disrupt his form, and his scoring streak continued in the Bundesliga and in European competition.

## POLE SCORER

Robert's debut for the national team came in September 2008, just after his 20th birthday. He came off the bench to score his first goal for Poland. EURO 2012 was Lewandowski's first major international tournament, and while the Eagles crashed out early on, the striker played in every game, scoring once. By 2014 he was captain of Poland and a regular goalscorer for his country. In World Cup qualification in 2017, Lewandowski moved on to 50 goals, as Poland topped their group. Russia 2018 was Poland's first appearance at the tournament for 12 years, with Lewandowski's goals in qualifying key to this achievement.

Lewandowski scored an amazing 16 goals in qualifying for the 2018 World Cup, a European record.

## ROB'S RECORDS

Lewandowski spent four seasons with Dortmund, scoring over 100 goals in fewer than 200 appearances. His 74 league goals were key to the club becoming German champions twice. In January 2014 however, the striker left for Bayern Munich on a free transfer. Robert continued his brilliant career there, winning the title three times as well as one German Cup and two Super Cups. He once scored five goals for Bayern despite only playing the second half – talk about a super sub! He also recorded the fastest Bundesliga hat-trick (3 minutes 22 seconds) as part of his five-goal haul.

**FOOTIE FACT**

***Robert comes from a sporting family – his father was a Polish judo champion and footballer, and his mother and sister have been professional volleyball players.***

# ROMELU LUKAKU

This **RED-HOT STRIKER** has a goalscoring record envied by almost every forward in the game. At just 24, he's already passed the 150-goal mark. He's a strong, **CLINICAL FINISHER** who can use his head as well as both feet. He uses his **POWERFUL** physique and acceleration to turn in plenty of world-class performances for club and country.

**MANCHESTER UNITED**

**FORWARD**

**FULL NAME:** Romelu Menama Lukaku Bolingoli

**NICKNAME:** The Lawyer

**DATE OF BIRTH:** 13 May 1993

**PLACE OF BIRTH:** Antwerp, Belgium

**HEIGHT:** 1.90m **WEIGHT:** 94kg

**LEFT OR RIGHT FOOTED:** Both

**SQUAD NUMBER:** 9

**INTERNATIONAL TEAM:** Belgium

## GOAL MACHINE

A teenage Lukaku made a name for himself at Anderlecht's academy in Belgium. His goal record was so good – 131 goals in 93 games – that he was promoted to the first team aged 16. After scoring 41 goals from 98 matches, Chelsea paid £18 million for the young Belgian. Loan spells at West Brom and Everton saw Lukaku really hit form, a period that convinced Everton to pay a club-record £28 million for the striker in 2014. The goals kept coming and Lukaku was hot property. In the summer of 2017 Manchester United beat Romelu's old club Chelsea to his signature, landing him for a massive initial fee of £75 million.

## STAR QUALITY

Lukaku leads the line for his country in a star-studded Belgium team that includes Eden Hazard, Thibaut Courtois and Kevin de Bruyne. He's hit the back of the net 31 times for Belgium since making his senior debut in 2010, and is already the Red Devils' record goalscorer aged just 24. In qualifying for Russia 2018, Romelu scored 11 goals in just eight games – only Robert Lewandowski and Cristiano Ronaldo struck more than him in the European qualifying groups.

## RED DEVIL

Lukaku is Manchester United's second-most expensive player of all time, behind team-mate Paul Pogba, and he is the most expensive striker in Premier League history. José Mourinho made Lukaku his number 9, a shirt previously worn by Zlatan Ibrahimović and Andrew Cole, and is hoping his star striker will deliver another Premier League title – United have not won the league since 2013. Romelu scored on his first start for the club – a UEFA Super Cup defeat to Real Madrid – and twice on his league debut.

Russia 2018 was Lukaku's second FIFA World Cup.

### FOOTIE FACT

***Despite his awesome goal record, Lukaku has won just one trophy in England – the FA Cup with Chelsea in 2012. The ambitious striker has his eye on more silverware.***

# MARCELO

A solid and **SPEEDY DEFENDER**, Marcelo loves to help his teams attack. His all-round game is so **IMPRESSIVE** that no other left-back playing today can match his ability. Marcelo was transported from Rio to the riches of Real Madrid, and is second only to Roberto Carlos for the number of matches played by an overseas player at the club. He's an **IMPORTANT** import!

## REAL MADRID

### DEFENDER

**FULL NAME:** Marcelo Vieira da Silva Júnior

**NICKNAME:** El Loco (The Crazy)

**DATE OF BIRTH:** 12 May 1988

**PLACE OF BIRTH:** Rio de Janeiro, Brazil

**HEIGHT:** 1.74m **WEIGHT:** 80kg

**LEFT OR RIGHT FOOTED:** Left

**SQUAD NUMBER:** 12

**INTERNATIONAL TEAM:** Brazil

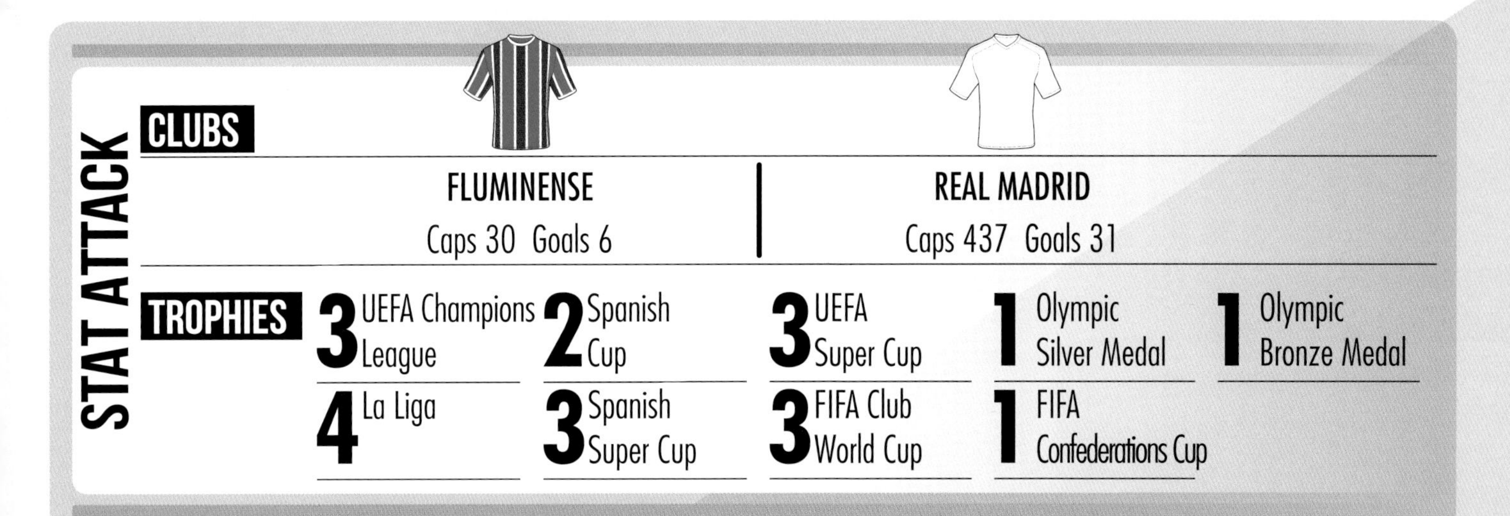

STAT ATTACK

CLUBS

| FLUMINENSE | REAL MADRID |
|---|---|
| Caps 30 Goals 6 | Caps 437 Goals 31 |

TROPHIES

3 UEFA Champions League
2 Spanish Cup
3 UEFA Super Cup
1 Olympic Silver Medal
1 Olympic Bronze Medal
4 La Liga
3 Spanish Super Cup
3 FIFA Club World Cup
1 FIFA Confederations Cup

## BRAZILIAN BORN

Marcelo grew up in a poor area of Rio de Janeiro in Brazil. His father was a firefighter and his mother a teacher, but Marcelo had no wish to follow in their footsteps – all he wanted to do was play football. Playing a mix of street football and futsal at the beach helped Marcelo develop his skills, and he signed for Fluminense's youth side aged 13. Marcelo became known as a fast, attacking and hardworking full-back. When Real Madrid's scouts watched him play in 2007, half of Europe's top clubs wanted him, but Real won his signature and Marcelo arrived in Spain in the January transfer window.

## REAL WINNER

Marcelo made Madrid's first 11 straightaway at left-back. But after a couple of poor seasons playing out of position, Marcelo's breakthrough came in 2010–11. New manager José Mourinho returned him to left-back and, by the end of that season, some said he was as valuable as Ronaldo and Messi. As the 2016–17 season ended, Marcelo had won 18 major trophies with Real Madrid, including four La Liga titles and a treble of UEFA Champions League wins, all before the age of 30.

## SAMBA STYLE

Marcelo has won almost 50 caps for Brazil and scored six goals, playing for his country for over a decade. He has won two Olympic medals – a bronze in 2008 and a silver in 2012 – as well as the 2013 FIFA Confederations Cup. When Brazil lost to Germany in a crushing 7–1 semi-final defeat at the World Cup in 2014, Marcelo called it the worst day of his career. Four years on, the defender is in the form of his life.

Marcelo is often compared to Roberto Carlos, another legendary Brazilian left-back. Many experts say Marcelo is even better!

### FOOTIE FACT

***Marcelo's best friends in football are his Real Madrid team-mate Cristiano Ronaldo and the Brazil defender Pepe.***

# LIONEL MESSI

In a world of football superstars, mini **MAGICIAN** Messi is a megastar. He's been at the top of his game since debuting for Barcelona in 2004, and will go down in history as one of football's all-time greats. His silverware collection is **SECOND TO NONE**, with four UEFA Champions League titles and eight La Liga trophies. He's a deadly dribbler with a **LETHAL LEFT FOOT** and scores goals for fun for both Barcelona and Argentina.

**BARCELONA**

**FORWARD**

**FULL NAME:** Lionel Andrés Messi Cuccittini

**NICKNAME:** La Pulga (The Flea)

**DATE OF BIRTH:** 24 June 1987

**PLACE OF BIRTH:** Rosario, Argentina

**HEIGHT:** 1.70m **WEIGHT:** 72kg

**LEFT OR RIGHT FOOTED:** Left

**SQUAD NUMBER:** 10

**INTERNATIONAL TEAM:** Argentina

## STAT ATTACK

**CLUBS**

| BARCELONA C | BARCELONA B | BARCELONA |
|---|---|---|
| Caps 10 Goals 5 | Caps 22 Goals 6 | Caps 619 Goals 534 |

**TROPHIES**

| | |
|---|---|
| 4 | UEFA Champions League |
| 5 | Spanish Cup |
| 3 | UEFA Super Cup |
| 3 | FIFA Club World Cup |
| 1 | Olympic Gold Medal |
| 8 | La Liga |
| 7 | Spanish Super Cup |

## STAR QUALITY

Growing up in Argentina, Messi started playing football from an early age. He was always smaller than his team-mates, but that didn't stop him. At the age of ten, he was told that his body was not growing normally and he needed medical treatment. Barcelona agreed to pay for his treatment and Messi moved with his family to Spain. By the age of 14, Messi was part of Barcelona's greatest-ever youth side and his talent was clear to everyone who saw him play. Messi played his first game for Barça's senior side, a friendly in late 2003, aged just 16 years and four months.

## REAL RIVALRY

The best player in Barcelona's history? His individual records are too long to list, but Messi is responsible for much of Barcelona's spectacular success in recent years. He has broken almost every club and La Liga record going, winning four UEFA Champions Leagues and 30 trophies overall with the Catalan club. A fifth Champions League win would make Messi the most successful non-European player in the competition's history. Messi's greatest rival is Real Madrid's Cristiano Ronaldo. The pair have battled it out between them to win the Ballon d'Or trophy five times each in the last ten years.

## AWESOME ARGENTINE

While Messi has won trophy after trophy at Barcelona, his Argentina side has not been so successful. Messi has been on the losing side with Argentina in four major finals, going out on penalties twice. He even retired for a while following the 2016 loss to Chile in the Copa América! His only senior trophy won with his country was a gold medal at the 2008 Olympic Games.

Messi is Argentina's top scorer of all time, with 61 goals by the end of qualifying for Russia 2018.

## FOOTIE FACT

***In 2012, Messi scored an unbelievable 91 goals combined in all competitions for Barcelona and Argentina. What a record!***

# MANUEL NEUER

Football experts agree that Neuer is one of the best keepers of all time. The World-Cup-winning **SHOT-STOPPER** has incredible reflexes and an excellent ability to read the game. He's a **COMMANDING FIGURE** in his penalty area and will rush out of the box to sweep up opposition attacks when needed. A **LEGENDARY LEADER**, Neuer is captain of both Bayern and Germany.

## BAYERN MUNICH

### GOALKEEPER

**FULL NAME:** Manuel Peter Neuer

**NICKNAMES:** Snapper, Manu

**DATE OF BIRTH:** 27 March 1986

**PLACE OF BIRTH:** Gelsenkirchen, West Germany

**HEIGHT:** 1.93m **WEIGHT:** 92kg

**LEFT OR RIGHT FOOTED:** Right

**SQUAD NUMBER:** 1

**INTERNATIONAL TEAM:** Germany

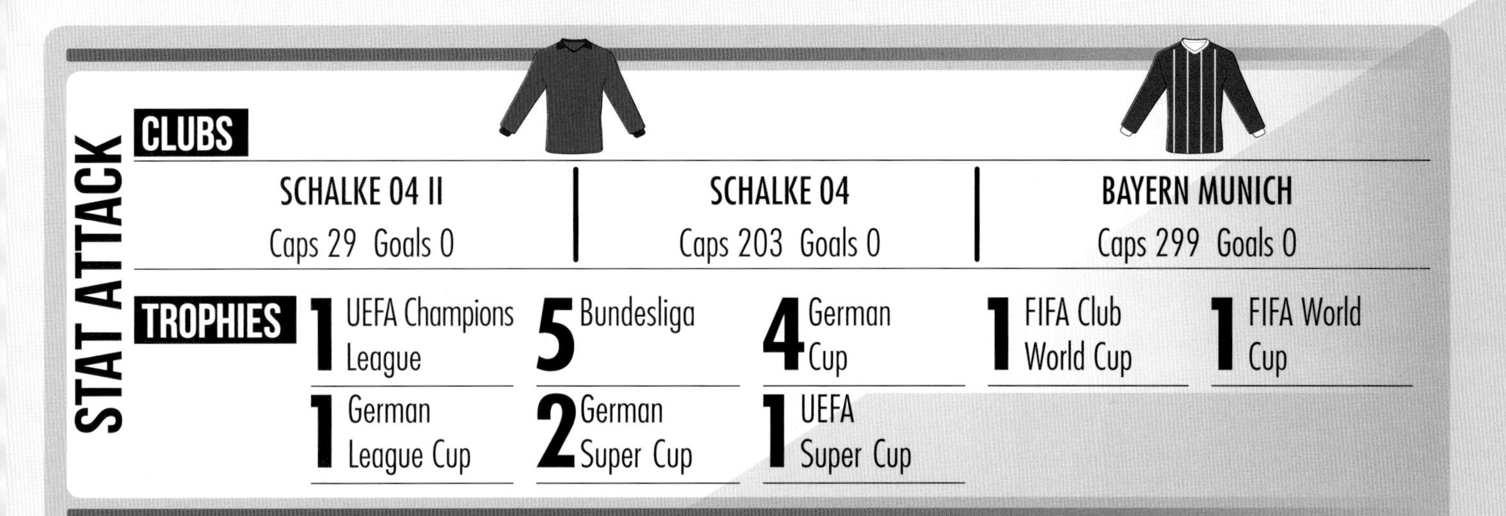

## STAT ATTACK

**CLUBS**

| SCHALKE 04 II | SCHALKE 04 | BAYERN MUNICH |
| --- | --- | --- |
| Caps 29 Goals 0 | Caps 203 Goals 0 | Caps 299 Goals 0 |

**TROPHIES**

- 1 UEFA Champions League
- 5 Bundesliga
- 4 German Cup
- 1 FIFA Club World Cup
- 1 FIFA World Cup
- 1 German League Cup
- 2 German Super Cup
- 1 UEFA Super Cup

# SCHALKE START

Manuel started playing football when he was four and later joined his hometown club, Schalke 04. At first he played outfield, but wanted to copy his idol Jens Lehmann and so he became a goalkeeper. He started out with the club's second team in the 2003–04 season, but by 2006–07 had become a first-team regular. Brilliant at commanding his defence and a standout shot-shopper, Neuer helped Schalke win two trophies. At the end of the 2010–11 season, Schalke reached the UEFA Champions League semi-finals, but lost to Manchester United. Hungry for success, Neuer announced he was moving to rivals Bayern Munich.

# WORLD-CUP WINNER

The Munich man made his debut for Germany in 2009 and was first-choice keeper for the 2010 World Cup, when they reached the semi-finals. The 2014 World Cup was the highlight of Neuer's international career so far. Playing as a 'sweeper-keeper', he helped Germany attack further up the pitch. A clean sheet in the final saw Germany beat Argentina to take the trophy, and Neuer was awarded the Golden Glove for the best goalkeeper in the tournament. That year, he finished third in the Ballon d'Or voting, behind Messi and Ronaldo.

# BAYERN'S BEST

In his first season at Bayern, Neuer went 1,000 minutes without conceding a goal, breaking the club record for the most competitive clean sheets in a row. His reputation grew following the Champions League final in 2012 when Neuer himself scored in the penalty shoot-out, but ultimately lost to Chelsea. A year later, Bayern were back in the UEFA Champions League final, and this time they beat Borussia Dortmund. Neuer and Bayern went on to dominate German football, winning a record-breaking five Bundesliga titles in a row, with league and cup doubles in 2012–13, 2013–14 and 2015–16.

Neuer has been voted the World's Best Goalkeeper and UEFA Goalkeeper of the Year eight times altogether.

## FOOTIE FACT

***Neuer was the voice for character Frank McCay in the German version of the 2013 animated movie Monsters University – strange but true!***

# NEYMAR

From playing barefoot on the backstreets of São Paulo to his £198-million **WORLD-RECORD TRANSFER** to Paris Saint-Germain, Neymar's journey to football stardom has been nothing short of incredible. The **BOY FROM BRAZIL** has established himself as one of the game's brightest stars, winning a host of trophies for **CLUB AND COUNTRY**.

## PARIS SAINT-GERMAIN

### FORWARD

**FULL NAME:** Neymar da Silva Santos Júnior

**NICKNAMES:** O Joia (The Gem), NJR

**DATE OF BIRTH:** 5 February 1992

**PLACE OF BIRTH:** São Paulo, Brazil

**HEIGHT:** 1.75m **WEIGHT:** 68kg

**LEFT OR RIGHT FOOTED:** Both

**SQUAD NUMBER:** 10

**INTERNATIONAL TEAM:** Brazil

STAT ATTACK

CLUBS

| SANTOS | BARCELONA | PARIS SAINT-GERMAIN |
|---|---|---|
| Caps 223 Goals 136 | Caps 186 Goals 105 | Caps 28 Goals 28 |

TROPHIES

| | | | | |
|---|---|---|---|---|
| 1 UEFA Champions League | 3 Spanish Cup | 1 FIFA Confederations Cup | 1 Brazilian Cup | 1 Recopa Sudamericana |
| 2 La Liga | 1 Spanish Super Cup | 1 FIFA Club World Cup | 1 Copa Libertadores | 1 Olympic Gold Medal |

## STREET STAR

The son of a professional footballer, Neymar was best friends with a ball from the age of two. He grew up playing street football and futsal, which helped him sharpen his skills and tricks. He was spotted by Santos FC and joined their youth team when he was only 11 years old and soon made a big impression as a dazzling forward and regular goalscorer. He almost signed for Real Madrid at the age of 14, but stayed with Santos for another five years, before switching to Spanish football in 2013 to join Catalan giants Barcelona.

## BARÇA BOYS

In his four seasons at Camp Nou, Neymar formed part of what is considered by many to be the greatest strike force in football history. When the thrilling trio of Lionel Messi, Luis Suárez and Neymar, nicknamed MSN, lined up together for Barça from 2013–17, the Catalan giants were almost unbeatable, winning an amazing nine trophies, including the domestic Treble in 2015. Neymar's individual stats for Barcelona are astonishing – 105 goals scored and 59 assists in just 186 appearances.

## MASSIVE MOVE

Following UEFA Champions League, La Liga, Spanish Cup and FIFA Club World Cup wins with Barça, Neymar was ready to step out of Messi's shadow at the start of the 2017–18 season and take on a fresh challenge. Paris Saint-Germain triggered the mega £198-million ($263-million) release clause in Neymar's contract, handing him the no.10 shirt once worn by Zlatan Ibrahimović. He kicked off his PSG career in style, scoring 28 goals in his first 28 league matches!

Neymar scored his 50th international goal for Brazil against Argentina, aged just 24.

## FOOTIE FACT

***Neymar follows in the footsteps of Brazil legends Romário, Ronaldo and Rivaldo, who all started out playing street football in bare feet. Neymar's heroes won four World Cups between them.***

# SERGIO RAMOS

Real Madrid's **FAMOUS NUMBER 4**, Sergio Ramos captains both his country and his club side. The **CLASSY CENTRE-BACK** makes very few mistakes and loves to get forward. He's famous for scoring late goals despite the fact he's a centre-back! Ramos hit a **DOUBLE-FIGURE** goal tally for the first time in 2016–17, a season when Madrid won La Liga and the UEFA Champions League.

## REAL MADRID

### DEFENDER

**FULL NAME:** Sergio Ramos García
**NICKNAME:** Cuqui (Cookie)
**DATE OF BIRTH:** 30 March 1986
**PLACE OF BIRTH:** Camas, Spain
**HEIGHT:** 1.84m **WEIGHT:** 82kg
**LEFT OR RIGHT FOOTED:** Right
**SQUAD NUMBER:** 4
**INTERNATIONAL TEAM:** Spain

STAT ATTACK

CLUBS

| SEVILLA | REAL MADRID |
|---|---|
| Caps: 50 Goals 3 | Caps: 548 Goals 70 |

TROPHIES

3 Champions League
2 Spanish Cup
3 UEFA Super Cup
1 FIFA World Cup
2 UEFA European Championship
4 La Liga
3 Spanish Super Cup
3 FIFA Club World Cup

## SEVILLA START

Ramos didn't always dream of being a footballer – his ambition was to be a bullfighter! Ramos' parents did not want him to get involved in such a dangerous sport. Instead, his brother encouraged him to try football and Ramos' natural talent was revealed. He joined Sevilla's youth team aged ten, and climbed the ranks until his first-team debut in February 2004. Ramos made 50 appearances for the club where he showed he could play as both a ferocious full-back and a strong central defender. After three seasons at Sevilla, Ramos was a wanted man.

## MADRID MOVE

Ramos moved to Madrid for £18 million in 2005, a record for a Spanish teenager. Winning La Liga in 2007 was the first of an amazing 18 trophies with Real. 2016–17 was a brilliant season for Ramos – he led Real to a league and UEFA Champions League double, becoming the first man to captain his club to back-to-back Champions League wins. While Ramos is a fantastic defender, he has been sent off 24 times in total for Real (19 times in La Liga, which is a league record), though his reputation is for silly rather than deliberate fouls.

## REIGNING FOR SPAIN

Ramos earned his first senior international cap just before turning 19, making him Spain's youngest player in 55 years. EURO 2008 was the first major tournament Ramos won with Spain, as the team entered a golden era of football. Made captain for the 2010 World Cup, Ramos started every game in South Africa, where Spain beat the Netherlands to be crowned World Champions. Another victorious tournament followed at EURO 2012. In 2013, he became Spain's youngest player to win 100 caps.

Ramos has enjoyed a glittering international career with Spain.

## FOOTIE FACT

*Ramos was once one of La Liga's fastest players and has clocked a sprinting speed of 30.6km per hour.*

# CRISTIANO RONALDO

After winning a record-equalling **FIFTH BALLON D'OR** award in December 2017, Ronaldo has said he believes he is the **BEST PLAYER** in football history. An unstoppable forward, Ronaldo has a trophy cabinet that any football player would envy, having won over **20 CLUB TROPHIES**, a EURO 2016 win with Portugal and a ton of individual awards – there are too many of Ron's records to mention!

**REAL MADRID**

**FORWARD**

**FULL NAME:** Cristiano Ronaldo dos Santos Aveiro
**NICKNAMES:** Ronnie, CR7
**DATE OF BIRTH:** 5 February 1985
**PLACE OF BIRTH:** Funchal, Madeira, Portugal
**HEIGHT:** 1.87m **WEIGHT:** 84kg
**LEFT OR RIGHT FOOTED:** Both
**SQUAD NUMBER:** 7
**INTERNATIONAL TEAM:** Portugal

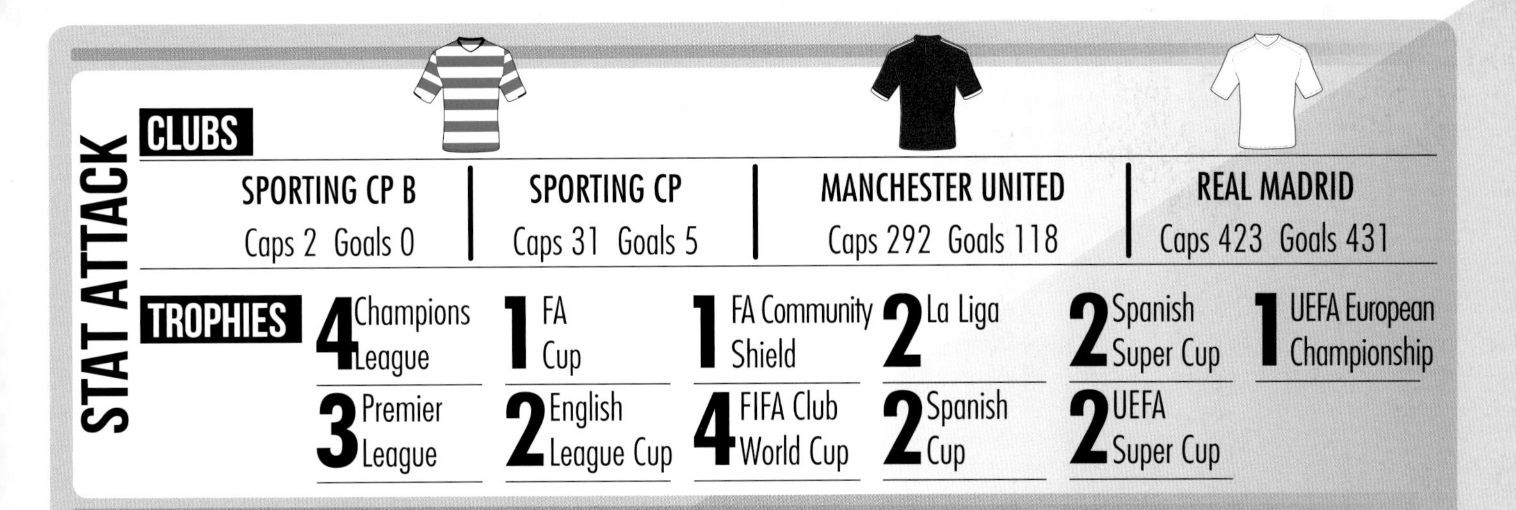

STAT ATTACK

CLUBS

| SPORTING CP B | SPORTING CP | MANCHESTER UNITED | REAL MADRID |
|---|---|---|---|
| Caps 2 Goals 0 | Caps 31 Goals 5 | Caps 292 Goals 118 | Caps 423 Goals 431 |

TROPHIES

| | | | | | |
|---|---|---|---|---|---|
| 4 Champions League | 1 FA Cup | 1 FA Community Shield | 2 La Liga | 2 Spanish Super Cup | 1 UEFA European Championship |
| 3 Premier League | 2 English League Cup | 4 FIFA Club World Cup | 2 Spanish Cup | 2 UEFA Super Cup | |

## TEENAGE SENSATION

Ronaldo made his first-team debut aged 17 at Sporting CP. But with a host of clubs interested in the young winger, he did not stay in Lisbon for long. A 2003 move to Manchester United for £12.24 million made him the most expensive teenager in English football history at the time. There, he was given the number 7 shirt, which was available following David Beckham's transfer to Real Madrid. During his time at United, Ronaldo tore up English football – the goals flowed and his top-scoring season was 2007–08, when his 42 goals helped the Red Devils to the UEFA Champions League title as well as the second of the three league titles Ronaldo won with the club.

## CAPTAIN CRISTIANO

Ronaldo earned his first senior cap for Portugal aged 18 and made the EURO 2004 squad a year later. It was the first of eight major tournaments in which Ronaldo has appeared. One day after his 22nd birthday, in February 2007, Ronaldo captained Portugal for the first time, a role that he still holds. His 50th international goal made him the first Portuguese to play and score in three World Cups, and he is now easily the country's all-time top scorer with 79 goals. Ronaldo's biggest achievement with Portugal was to captain the side to their first-ever victory in a major tournament at EURO 2016 in France.

As well as being Portugal's leading scorer, Ronaldo is the country's most-capped player.

## FIRST-CLASS FORWARD

Hungry for more honours, Ronaldo moved to Real Madrid for a then world-record fee of £80 million. His debut season ended without a trophy, but Ronaldo still scored 33 goals. Since then he has won back-to-back Champions Leagues, two La Liga titles and been named as the world's best player. Being able to score with either foot, his head and from set pieces saw Ronaldo rack up a jaw-dropping 61 goals in 2014–15. He can create goals, too, and holds the record for the all-time number of assists in the UEFA Champions League, a competition in which he has scored over 100 goals.

### FOOTIE FACT

***Ronaldo is so famous that he even has an airport named after him in Madeira, Portugal, the island where he grew up.***

# ALEXIS SÁNCHEZ

Manchester United's Alexis is a fast, **CREATIVE** and hardworking attacker, who can play anywhere along the forward line. He's naturally right-footed, but **SCORES FOR FUN** with both feet. His goals for former club Arsenal helped them win two FA Cups before a mega move to Manchester United went through in January 2018. One of the Premier League's **BEST FINISHERS**, any top club would be happy to have Sánchez in their squad.

MANCHESTER UNITED

**FORWARD**

**FULL NAME:** Alexis Alejandro Sánchez Sánchez

**NICKNAMES:** El Niño Maravilla (The Boy Wonder), La Ardilla (The Squirrel)

**DATE OF BIRTH:** 19 December 1988

**PLACE OF BIRTH:** Tocopilla, Chile

**HEIGHT:** 1.69m **WEIGHT:** 62kg

**LEFT OR RIGHT FOOTED:** Both

**SQUAD NUMBER:** 7

**INTERNATIONAL TEAM:** Chile

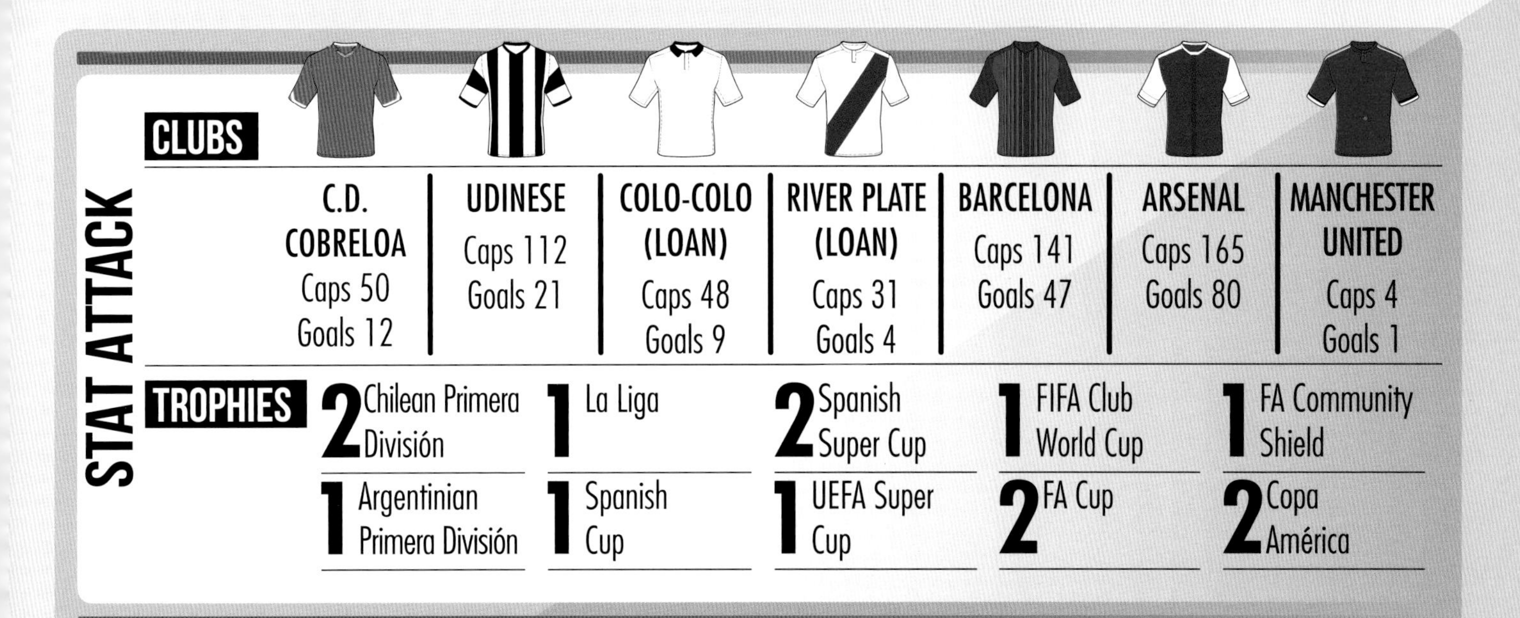

STAT ATTACK

CLUBS

| C.D. COBRELOA | UDINESE | COLO-COLO (LOAN) | RIVER PLATE (LOAN) | BARCELONA | ARSENAL | MANCHESTER UNITED |
|---|---|---|---|---|---|---|
| Caps 50<br>Goals 12 | Caps 112<br>Goals 21 | Caps 48<br>Goals 9 | Caps 31<br>Goals 4 | Caps 141<br>Goals 47 | Caps 165<br>Goals 80 | Caps 4<br>Goals 1 |

TROPHIES

| | | | | |
|---|---|---|---|---|
| 2 Chilean Primera División | 1 La Liga | 2 Spanish Super Cup | 1 FIFA Club World Cup | 1 FA Community Shield |
| 1 Argentinian Primera División | 1 Spanish Cup | 1 UEFA Super Cup | 2 FA Cup | 2 Copa América |

## ALEXIS ON THE MOVE

Sánchez began his career at Chilean club Cobreloa, before moving to Serie A's Udinese in 2006. After two loan spells – in Chile and Argentina – and three impressive seasons at Udinese, Barcelona came in with a £22-million offer. In his second season with Barça, Sánchez showed what he could do in front of goal, scoring eight league goals to help win La Liga. 2013–14 saw Alexis net 21 goals in total, his best season tally to date, but it was to be his last campaign in Spain.

## RECORD BREAKER

Sánchez made his debut for Chile in 2006 and has since won 119 caps for his country, making him the joint most-capped Chilean player of all-time, alongside keeper Claudio Bravo. He's also Chile's record goalscorer, having netted for his country 39 times. His goals have been crucial in helping Chile win the Copa América twice, in 2015 and 2016, and they also reached the final of the 2017 FIFA Confederations Cup.

Chile did not make it to the 2018 FIFA World Cup but appeared in the two previous tournaments.

## PREMIER PLAYER

Sánchez moved again in summer 2014, this time to Arsenal for a mega £31.7 million. He lit up the Premier League in his debut season, netting 16 league goals. He scored more goals at Wembley than any other Arsenal player and in 2017 he struck the Gunners' fastest-ever FA Cup final goal after just 229 seconds. He left Arsenal in search of more trophies with Manchester United in January 2018, in a straight swap for Henrikh Mkhitaryan in a deadline-day deal. He's the first Chilean to play and score for the Red Devils and already feels at home at Old Trafford.

### FOOTIE FACT

***Sánchez has won trophies in four different countries – Chile, Argentina, Spain and England. He really is a world beater!***

# LUIS SUÁREZ

A stunning striker, Suárez has an unbelievable record of career goals with over **350 STRIKES** for five clubs in four different countries – wherever he's played he's scored! His journey from sweeping the streets in Uruguay to earn money for his family, to becoming one of **BARCELONA'S BEST** reads like a footballing fairy-tale. He's a **TRUE LEGEND** of the game.

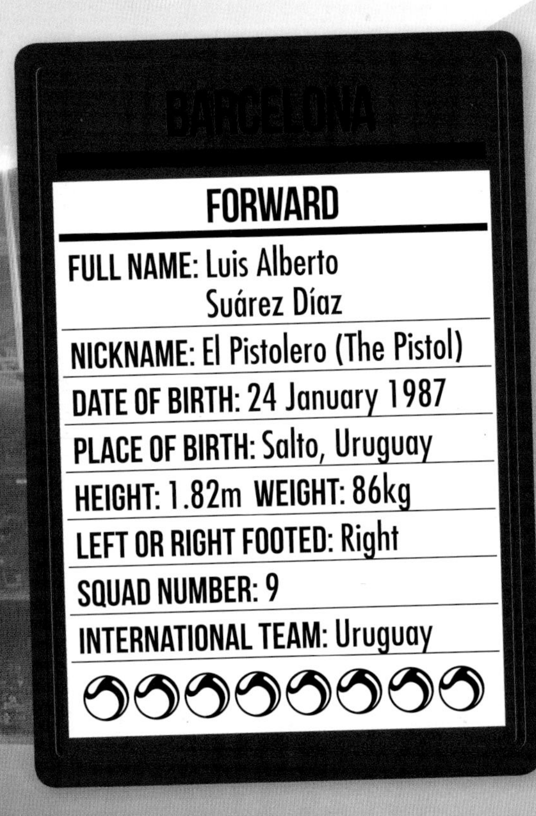

BARCELONA

**FORWARD**

**FULL NAME:** Luis Alberto Suárez Díaz

**NICKNAME:** El Pistolero (The Pistol)

**DATE OF BIRTH:** 24 January 1987

**PLACE OF BIRTH:** Salto, Uruguay

**HEIGHT:** 1.82m **WEIGHT:** 86kg

**LEFT OR RIGHT FOOTED:** Right

**SQUAD NUMBER:** 9

**INTERNATIONAL TEAM:** Uruguay

STAT ATTACK

CLUBS

| | NACIONAL | GRONINGEN | AJAX | LIVERPOOL | BARCELONA |
|---|---|---|---|---|---|
| Caps | 34 | 37 | 159 | 133 | 176 |
| Goals | 12 | 15 | 111 | 82 | 140 |

TROPHIES

| NACIONAL | GRONINGEN | AJAX | LIVERPOOL | BARCELONA |
|---|---|---|---|---|
| 1 Uruguayan Primera División | 1 Dutch Cup | 2 La Liga | 1 Spanish Super Cup | 1 UEFA Super Cup |
| 1 Dutch Eredivisie | 1 English League Cup | 3 Spanish Cup | 1 UEFA Champions League | 1 FIFA Club World Cup |

# TOUGH CHILDHOOD

Suárez is from Uruguay, a country with just 3.5 million people and where football brings the nation together. He began playing barefoot on the cobbled streets of his hometown, Salto. His family were poor, and Suárez did not even have his own boots. His tough start in life made him hungry for success. He won the league with Nacional aged 19, before being snapped up by Dutch club Groningen. After a single season there, Ajax made a move for the forward and Suárez went on to star for the Amsterdam club for three and a half seasons.

# REDS CAREER

Suárez joined Liverpool in January 2011 for £22.8 million and was given the legendary number 7 shirt. By May 2013 he had established himself as one of Europe's top strikers and scored 30 goals that season. The following season was better still, when the Reds finished as runners-up in the Premier League. Suárez scored an incredible 31 goals in 37 matches, winning the Premier League Golden Boot and the Player of the Season award. The ambitious forward left Liverpool having scored 82 goals, but with only the League Cup trophy to show for his efforts.

# BEST FORM

Since his £65-million move to Barcelona in 2014, Suárez has gone from strength to strength. He won a league and UEFA Champions League double in his first season at the Nou Camp and contributed 25 goals and 20 assists in all competitions. Before Neymar left for PSG, Suárez, Messi and Neymar formed perhaps the deadliest attacking trio in football history. In his first 100 matches for Barcelona, Suárez scored more goals and made more assists in Spain than both Cristiano Ronaldo and Lionel Messi managed in the same number of games – that's some record!

Suárez is a real team player, as shown by his five goals and seven assists in qualifying for Russia 2018.

## FOOTIE FACT

***While Suárez is a talented footballer, he has a bad-boy reputation. His long bans have taken some of the shine off a brilliant career.***

# YOUNG GUNS

Now you know which players made the grade as the superstars of world football, it's time to showcase the skills of the next generation. Big things are predicted for these youngsters over the next decade, with some of them already starring for club and country. Take a look at our selection of top talent from a commanding keeper to some sensational strikers.

## TAMMY ABRAHAM

A Chelsea player since he was seven, goals have always been key to Abraham's game. The strong, physical centre-forward has averaged a goal in every other game in his senior career so far. Loaned to Swansea for the 2017–18 season, Abraham has made important first-team appearances and earned his first England cap.

### SWANSEA CITY

**FORWARD**

**DATE OF BIRTH:** 2 October 1997
**PLACE OF BIRTH:** London
**HEIGHT:** 1.90m **WEIGHT:** 80kg
**LEFT OR RIGHT FOOTED:** Right
**SQUAD NUMBER:** 10
**INTERNATIONAL TEAM:** England
**DOMESTIC APPEARANCES:** 76; **GOALS:** 33

## OUSMANE DEMBÉLÉ

Barcelona believed Dembélé to be one of the game's hottest prospects and brought him in for a fee of around £97 million to replace Neymar – making him the joint-second most expensive player in history (with Paul Pogba). The young forward has pace and can use both feet to devastating effect when fully fit. Unfortunately, injury limited his appearances in his debut La Liga season.

### BARCELONA

**FORWARD**

**DATE OF BIRTH:** 15 May 1997
**PLACE OF BIRTH:** Vernon, France
**HEIGHT:** 1.78m **WEIGHT:** 73kg
**LEFT OR RIGHT FOOTED:** Both
**SQUAD NUMBER:** 11
**INTERNATIONAL TEAM:** France
**DOMESTIC APPEARANCES:** 109; **GOALS:** 35

## GIANLUIGI **DONNARUMMA**

Donnarumma debuted for AC Milan's first team as a 16-year-old – almost unheard of for a keeper! He kept 31 clean sheets in his first 92 Serie A matches and made a penalty shoot-out save to secure the club's first trophy in five seasons – the 2016 Italian Super Cup. Now Gianluigi Buffon has retired from international football, Italy's no.1 shirt should easily belong to him.

### AC MILAN

**GOALKEEPER**

**DATE OF BIRTH:** 25 February 1999
**PLACE OF BIRTH:** Castellammare di Stabia, Italy
**HEIGHT:** 1.96m **WEIGHT:** 90kg
**LEFT OR RIGHT FOOTED:** Right
**SQUAD NUMBER:** 99
**INTERNATIONAL TEAM:** Italy
**DOMESTIC APPEARANCES:** 106

## TIMOTHY **FOSU-MENSAH**

On a season-long loan from Manchester United to Crystal Palace in 2017–18, intelligent defender Fosu-Mensah showed he can play as a centre-half or full-back as well as in midfield. His speed allows him to keep up with any forward, while his strength and physical qualities have earned him his first caps with the Netherlands. While Fosu-Mensah admits he still has a lot to learn, his future looks bright.

### CRYSTAL PALACE

**DEFENDER**

**DATE OF BIRTH:** 2 January 1998
**PLACE OF BIRTH:** Amsterdam, Netherlands
**HEIGHT:** 1.90m **WEIGHT:** 68kg
**LEFT OR RIGHT FOOTED:** Right
**SQUAD NUMBER:** 24
**INTERNATIONAL TEAM:** Netherlands
**DOMESTIC APPEARANCES:** 43; **GOALS:** 0

## GABRIEL **JESUS**

Jesus grew up playing street football in the Brazilian district of São Paulo and joined Manchester City in 2017 for a fee of £27 million. Some pundits have compared him to Lionel Messi at the same age – he can play in any attacking role and his creative and technical play are both incredible for such a young player. His stats for the Sky Blues and Brazil speak for themselves.

### MANCHESTER CITY

**FORWARD**

**DATE OF BIRTH:** 3 April 1997
**PLACE OF BIRTH:** São Paulo, Brazil
**HEIGHT:** 1.75m **WEIGHT:** 73kg
**LEFT OR RIGHT FOOTED:** Right
**SQUAD NUMBER:** 33
**INTERNATIONAL TEAM:** Brazil
**DOMESTIC APPEARANCES:** 121; **GOALS:** 45

## KYLIAN MBAPPÉ

Not many people had heard of Mbappé before the lightning-fast forward was picked up by Paris Saint-Germain on loan, but with a rumoured £160 million option to buy. In his first full season for Monaco, 2016–17, Mbappé had caught PSG's eye by scoring 15 goals on the way to the Ligue 1 title, plus six Champions League goals.

### PARIS SAINT-GERMAIN

**FORWARD**

**DATE OF BIRTH:** 20 December 1998
**PLACE OF BIRTH:** Paris, France
**HEIGHT:** 1.78m **WEIGHT:** 73kg
**LEFT OR RIGHT FOOTED:** Right
**SQUAD NUMBER:** 29
**INTERNATIONAL TEAM:** France
**DOMESTIC APPEARANCES:** 90; **GOALS:** 42

## CHRISTIAN PULISIC

Could this teenager be the USA's best-ever player? He's already played 50 games in the Bundesliga and is Borussia Dortmund's youngest-ever scorer in the UEFA Champions League. Cool under pressure, he can use both feet and may very well be the first world-class player to come out of the States. The fact that the USA failed to qualify for the 2018 FIFA World Cup will only drive Pulisic's ambition.

### BORUSSIA DORTMUND

**MIDFIELDER**

**DATE OF BIRTH:** 18 September 1998
**PLACE OF BIRTH:** Hershey, Pennsylvania, USA
**HEIGHT:** 1.73m **WEIGHT:** 63kg
**LEFT OR RIGHT FOOTED:** Both
**SQUAD NUMBER:** 22
**INTERNATIONAL TEAM:** USA
**DOMESTIC APPEARANCES:** 82; **GOALS:** 11

## MARCUS RASHFORD

Rashford burst on to the scene when he scored twice on his UEFA Europa League debut and twice again on his first Premier League start three days later. Since his opening strike for England, Rashford has become a full international. The exciting striker has won the FA Cup, League Cup and UEFA Europa League – all before his 20th birthday.

### MANCHESTER UNITED

**FORWARD**

**DATE OF BIRTH:** 31 October 1997
**PLACE OF BIRTH:** Manchester, England
**HEIGHT:** 1.80m **WEIGHT:** 70kg
**LEFT OR RIGHT FOOTED:** Right
**SQUAD NUMBER:** 19
**INTERNATIONAL TEAM:** England
**DOMESTIC APPEARANCES:** 108; **GOALS:** 29

## JADON SANCHO

Winger Sancho was in the World-Cup-winning England U17 squad in 2017. He was also crowned player of the tournament for his performances in the UEFA European U17 Championship earlier that year. He moved to Borussia Dortmund from Manchester City in search of first-team football and could be destined for great things in Germany.

### BORUSSIA DORTMUND

**ATTACKING MIDFIELDER**

**DATE OF BIRTH:** 25 March 2000
**PLACE OF BIRTH:** London, England
**HEIGHT:** 1.80m **WEIGHT:** 76kg
**LEFT OR RIGHT FOOTED:** Right
**SQUAD NUMBER:** 7
**INTERNATIONAL TEAM:** England
**DOMESTIC APPEARANCES:** 9; **GOALS:** 0

## THEO HERNÁNDEZ

Real Madrid's classy French left-back Theo Hernández is known simply as Theo. He moved across Madrid to join *Los Blancos* from Atlético in the summer of 2017 and made a handful of appearances in defence in his first season, as well as winning two trophies – the Spanish and UEFA Super Cups. His dream is to play for France's senior side, although he may be tempted by a call-up from Spain if one comes.

### REAL MADRID

**DEFENDER**

**DATE OF BIRTH:** 6 October 1997
**PLACE OF BIRTH:** Marseille, France
**HEIGHT:** 1.84m **WEIGHT:** 80kg
**LEFT OR RIGHT FOOTED:** Left
**SQUAD NUMBER:** 15
**INTERNATIONAL TEAM:** France
**DOMESTIC APPEARANCES:** 63; **GOALS:** 2

## THE BENCH

These super substitutes complete our Young Guns squad.

**DAVINSON SÁNCHEZ**
Tottenham & Colombia defender

**JUSTIN KLUIVERT**
Ajax midfielder

**YOURI TIELEMANS**
Anderlecht & Belgium midfielder

**FEDERICO CHIESA**
Fiorentina midfielder

**BEN WOODBURN**
Liverpool & Wales forward

# SUPERSTARS QUIZ

LOOK BACK THROUGH THE BOOK IF YOU GET STUCK.

Try this **SUPERSTARS QUIZ** on your own or with a footie friend to see who's top of the league. The answers are at the bottom of the page, but don't peek until you've finished answering all the questions.

**1** Whose club and country are both nicknamed 'The Red Devils'?

**A** Kevin de Bruyne
**B** Romelu Lukaku
**C** Eden Hazard

**2** Whose nickname is 'The Little Magician'?

**A** Philippe Coutinho
**B** Gabriel Jesus
**C** N'Golo Kanté

**3** Who is the only goalkeeper to feature in the Young Guns section?

**A** Manuel Neuer
**B** Gianluigi Donnarumma
**C** Jadon Sancho

**4** Which two players have won the Ballon d'Or prize a record five times each?

**A** Lionel Messi and Neymar
**B** Luis Suárez and Lionel Messi
**C** Lionel Messi and Cristiano Ronaldo

**5** What is the nickname of Barcelona's one-time legendary attacking force?

**A** MSN
**B** FCB
**C** The fearsome threesome

**6** For which national team does Luis Suárez play?

**A** Brazil
**B** Chile
**C** Uruguay

**7** In which position does Theo play for Real Madrid?

**A** Defence
**B** Midfield
**C** Forward

**8** Which of these midfielders began his career as a full-back?

**A** Dele Alli
**B** N'Golo Kanté
**C** Gareth Bale